SHIPS, BOATS AND CRAFT

SHIPS, BOATS AND CRAFT

SHIPS, BOATS AND CRAFT

by

STUART E. BECK

Illustrated by

THE AUTHOR and A. R. PAYNE

HERBERT JENKINS LIMITED
3 DUKE OF YORK STREET, ST. JAMES'S
LONDON, S.W. I

A
HERBERT
JENKINS
BOOK

First printing 1939
Reprinted . 1942

Printed in Great Britain by
Wyman and Sons, Ltd., London, Fakenham and Reading.

To

MY WIFE

who has patiently given up
countless hours of companion-
ship for the sake of this work

PREFACE

FOR as long as I can remember one of my chief delights has been to fossick around harbours, docks, and other places where ships lie, and in presenting this book it is my hope that the reader may capture some of the interest if not the thrill of such a pastime. Without making any claims for its comprehensiveness it would at least be no exaggeration to say that between these two covers will be found a more varied collection of craft than has been seen together in any port of the Seven Seas.

To facilitate the identification of any vessel by her appearance, the types have been divided, as far as possible, into several main groups. With a complicated subject of this kind, however, there are bound to be a number of 'border' cases which might be placed equally well in either of two sections. Consequently the grouping must not be taken as by any means a rigid classification, but rather a rough guide to the type of ship 'in sight.'

It will be appreciated that in the collection of data for a work of this nature far too many sources of information were utilized for me to acknowledge each one individually, but I take this opportunity to express my deep gratitude to all the museums, libraries, artists, writers and seafarers without whose invaluable assistance this volume would have remained for ever an unattainable dream.

C O N T E N T S

INTRODUCTION

IN any more or less general survey of the world's ships and craft from primitive times to the present day, at one end of the list will appear hollowed logs and rafts and at the other such mobile floating cities as the 'Queen Elizabeth' and the 'Queen Mary.' Poles apart though these examples may be, they have in common one fundamental purpose which holds good for vessels of every denomination. The primary object of the hollowed log was to carry man and his goods across a stretch of water that he could not otherwise negotiate; the same motive inspired the construction of the 'Queen Mary.' It is true that in the case of the early craft the stretch of water was probably no more than a stream compared with the oceans traversed by its modern counterpart, but the basic principle remains the same.

One of the most interesting aspects in the study of ships is to note the influence of local material on construction. To-day, of course, with the even distribution of steel and wood brought about by modern transport this is less apparent; but in earlier times it was a factor of primary importance. In places where there were forests producing suitable timber, wooden vessels of considerable size were to be found. On the other hand, where timber was scarce the ships would be of much less ambitious dimensions, and often such substitutes as wicker-work, animal skins, whalebone, etc., would be used.

Many thousands of improvements and inventions have contributed to the development of the world's ships in size, speed and seaworthiness. The use of multiple banks of oars in galleys and the introduction of triangular headsails, although widely separated in years, are two of the many which readily spring to mind. Others, very much more recent, which stand out in their effect on performance are the 'Clipper' hull-form, iron construction in the place of wood, and the advent of mechanical propulsion.

Another interesting sidelight is provided by the widely-differing rates of development in various parts of the world. In the days when European craft were still of a most primitive nature, the Chinese were employing seaworthy junks which frequently made long voyages and in some cases even water-tight compartments were fitted. Since then European vessels have passed through myriad phases resulting in the steam, oil, and motor-driven craft as we know them to-day; yet the junks of China remain unchanged, completely unaffected by the passage of time.

Modern 'business' vessels, as distinct from privately-owned pleasure craft such as may be found in any of the innumerable yachting centres throughout the world, may be divided into two main categories, quite apart from size, method of propulsion or location. First, and most familiar to the man in the street, is the class which lives by carrying either passengers or cargo. The second embraces all vessels that *work* afloat, and includes such craft as fishing vessels, cable ships, dredgers and warships. Although, with the exception of warships, this section of the community of ships is seldom in the limelight, it is nevertheless an important and extremely interesting one.

Finally, it should be pointed out that it does not come within the scope of this book to trace the evolution of shipping from the dim ages to the present day. The intervening centuries have produced so many types and modifications of these types that any work conceived on so ambitious a scale would fill volumes. For this reason the present work must be accepted as no more than a survey which diligent research and enthusiasm have made as comprehensive as possible.

HISTORICAL

HISTORICAL

THROUGHOUT the ages the building of ships has been governed by two important factors: the extent of man's knowledge of the subject at the time of construction and his ability to produce, within those limits, the most suitable craft for his purpose.

But in early times, as mentioned in the introduction, there was another factor of almost equal importance which has now largely disappeared—access to suitable materials. The ancient Egyptians, for instance, had no choice, but to use short thick planks of acacia wood in the building of their ships. They had none of the fine lengths of timber with which the Norsemen were favoured, and of necessity the shape and size of the vessels they constructed were governed very largely by the limitations of the material available.

Superstition in maritime history is as old as ships themselves. In the dim ages hapless slaves were sometimes crushed beneath the keels of galleys at their launch as propitiatory sacrifices to ensure good fortune for the ships. To-day, in certain fishing communities it is considered unlucky for the ballast from an old boat to be transferred to a new one; whilst, on the other side of the world, native craft still have eyes painted on their bows so that they may 'see' and thus steer a true course. Although, by comparison, the present day customs may seem less gruesome and bloody than of yore, in the hearts of men who follow the sea they are every bit as vital and important.

The ships of Columbus's day and long after were bad sailing craft; slow, unwieldy, and capable of sailing only with the wind almost astern. It is small wonder that casualties were many and that the bones of thousands of vessels littered the shores of the world during the Golden Age of Adventure. Yet the courage of the men who sailed in them was indomitable. Facing incredible hardships and the hazards of uncharted seas they laid the foundation to the magnificent tradition that has survived to this day.

H I S T O R I C A L

INDIAN STATE BARGE

This type varies greatly and it is only possible to give one example. She is a large punt-shaped vessel with high bow and stern, particularly the former which supports a throne and awning for the Maharana. The craft is propelled by sixteen oarsmen and steered with a great paddle.

ROYAL BARGE

Conveyed royalty, ambassadors and other important personages on river journeys. Varied considerably in size and design. The English example of 1689 was in use until comparatively recent times. She is an oak-built craft 40 ft. in length. Was used for travel between Windsor and Greenwich. Painted in scarlet and gold.

ENGLISH BATTLESHIP (17th Century)

Ships of this period still retained the lateen mizen, but had better lines and were much more seaworthy than the galleon type. The gilding and ornamentation were most elaborate and accounted for an appreciable proportion of the building cost. Typical dimensions: 130 ft. $\times$ 45 ft. 1,500 tons. 100 guns. Crew of about 780.

1st RATE LINE OF BATTLE SHIP

The largest type of war vessel afloat during the Nelson period. '1st Rates' were ships having 100 guns or over, arranged on three decks. Of deep draught and slow, but with most powerful armament of those days. '2nd Rates' were similar ships but with rather fewer guns.

BEURTMAN

A small Dutch cargo vessel, the example shown being in commission at the beginning of the 19th century. In deference to local conditions she is somewhat tubby and flat-bottomed, but stoutly built, as are the majority of Dutch vessels.

BLANKENBURG 'BRIG'

An open Belgian sailing lugger with two masts, one at the extreme bow forward-raked. The leeboards were long and narrow, almost vertical when lowered. Small sail area for her size. Employed as a fisherman off the mouth of the Schelde. Interesting detail is the bridle on mainsail.

COLLIER BRIG

These stout little vessels, nicknamed 'Geordies', were engaged in the coal trade from English N.E. coast ports during last century. Features were the straight stem without figurehead, and an exceptionally large jib. Manned by a crew of about six. Tonnage about 200 to 300. Approximate dimensions 100 ft. × 25 ft.

TRAINING BRIG

The brig is a two-masted vessel, completely square-rigged on both masts. For some time after the introduction of steam ships, the personnel of the British Navy were sail-trained, and the brig illustrated was one of five manned chiefly by boys from naval schools. Smart ships of about 500 tons.

BUCENTAUR

These gorgeous craft were State Galleys of Venice, in which the Doge annually 'married' the Adriatic. This particular vessel was built in 1729. More suitable for ceremony than for useful seafaring, she was elaborately ornamented, and had a long beak reminiscent of the more ancient war galley.

CARRACK

A three-masted merchant vessel, sailing the seas during the 15th and 16th centuries. Heavily built, beamy and bluff bowed. A clumsy sailer, but with her lateen mizen, a great advance on earlier ships. Although a trader, she carried top castles and other defensive measures against pirates and suchlike.

COPER

This type of vessel, originally Dutch, supplying clothes, etc., to Dogger Bank and other fishermen, deteriorated into a floating grog shop, in which smacksmen could exchange fish, gear and even boats for cheap spirit when forced to lie idle at sea through calms. The Coper was abolished about 1890.

CORVETTE

A fast, lightly-armed war vessel, more or less a miniature frigate. Generally ship-rigged and carried oars for propulsion in calms or for quick manœuvring in light airs. The oars were worked through small openings beside the gun ports. Single deck ships mounting about 20 guns.

REVENUE CUTTER

A small, cutter-rigged vessel employed by the Customs authorities to suppress smuggling. They were fast little craft, sometimes armed with 20 guns or so, and manned by large, well-picked crews. In size, the boats ranged between about 50 and 200 tons.

EAST INDIAMAN

Armed merchant vessels belonging to the famous East India Company. Superbly built and kept, they made huge profits for their owners. Carried a number of passengers. Varied in size, increasing until, in the early 19th century, they were of about 1,460 tons. The company went out of business about 1834.

EARLY EGYPTIAN SHIP

The ancient Egyptians were considerably handicapped in their shipbuilding by lack of timber of sufficient length. Their ships were built of short, thick planks of acacia wood joined together by dovetailed wedges. To get over longitudinal weakness a rope truss was used. The double mast was another feature.

THIRTEENTH-CENTURY SHIP

The lines of hull are similar to those of earlier vessels, also the mast and square sail, but castles are built over bow and stern. Ships varied in size, of course, but 80 or 90 ft. was an average length. Type of ships used in the Crusades.

ENGLISH SHIP (16th Century)

These Elizabethan vessels were contemporary with the Spanish galleon, but were rather smaller and handier when it came to quick manoeuvring. Later examples sometimes had four masts. A long false prow was fitted under the bowsprit. Steering was by whipstaff and tiller. About 700 to 800 tons.

FRIGATE

A ship whose position in the fleet was more or less equivalent to that of the modern cruiser. The first of this type was built in 1646. Her dimensions were approximately as follows : length 100 ft., beam 26 ft., depth 13 ft. She had an armament of 32 guns. Crew about 130 men.

FIRE SHIP

Small, inferior vessel of a fleet dismantled and filled with combustible material such as tar-barrels, gunpowder, etc. and all her guns loaded. She was then set on fire and allowed to drift down among the enemy ships. Drake used these craft in his defeat of the Armada.

GALLEASS

The galleass is larger than the galley, and relies very much more on her sails than on oars. The beak is a prominent feature. The galleass frequently had three masts and was lateen rigged. One of her advantages over the galley was that she could fire her guns broadside.

GALLEON

This high-built, unwieldy vessel was a development of the carrack. Three- or four-masted, with lateen mizen, and often square sail under bowsprit. Most famous of this type were those of the Spanish Main and Armada. Elaborately ornamented superstructure and tops. Mounted numerous guns and had large crews.

GALLEOT

A Dutch cargo vessel of considerable interest historically, being a forerunner of the bomb-ketch. Of typical Dutch hull design with apple bow and stern, the rig varied according to period, early examples setting a lateen sail on the mizen mast. The sketch shows a galleot of about 1850.

GREEK GALLEY

Among the earliest sea-going ships, galleys were divided into two main classes, namely, war galleys and merchant galleys. The former were full-bodied, propelled largely by sails. The latter were long narrow craft with rams and numerous oars for speed. The example shows an early Greek galley.

GUN-BOAT

A large open boat propelled by oars and with a swivel gun mounted in the bows. These craft were carried by large war vessels during the 18th and 19th century, and were used for landing and 'cutting out' expeditions. Carried a boat's crew and a number of marines.

HERRING BUSS

An early type of North Sea fishing vessel. Varied considerably, the one illustrated being at sea in the 16th century. As she was a drifter, the fore and main masts could be lowered, resting on special 'gallows'. She was a heavy, bluff-bowed ship of about 56 tons. Dimensions: 58 ft. × 15 ft.

'HOGGIE'

The Brighton Hog Boat or 'Hoggie' was an English South coast fishing vessel of the 18th and 19th centuries. With great beam, lee-boards and modified sprit rig she appears to have something of the Dutchman in her make-up. Has a heavy vertical transom stern and wide bilge keels.

HOY

A small 16th–19th century coaster working in British and Continental waters. Her sail plan comprised loose-footed mainsail, square top-sail, foresail and jib. Dimensions were roughly as follows: 80 ft. × 21 ft. × 12 ft. depth of hold. There are at least two English Inns named after these little ships.

KING'S SHIP

An early English vessel built for fighting. Called 'King's Shippes' because they belonged to the Crown, as distinct from the merchant ships which helped in defence. Had one mast with top-castle of lattice work, also high fore and after castles for fighting men. Manned by a crew of about 25 to 30 men.

SHIP'S LAUNCH (18th Century)

A stout open boat carried by large nava vessels. Employed, on occasion, in laying out anchors, etc., hence the barrel windlass amidships and short derrick aft for hauling or paying out cable. Fitted with mast and sail. The example is about 25 ft. long and 7 ft. beam.

ROMAN MERCHANT SHIP

The illustration shows a vessel of the 2nd century. She is a beamy, heavily-built ship of about 250 tons. Propelled entirely by sail, sometimes set a topsail. There were steering paddles either side of stern worked by tillers. Used for transport of grain from Egypt and Levant to Rome.

SLAVER

Many types of ships have been employed in this gruesome trade—schooners, dhows, etc., but all had to be fast sailers and well-armed. Although some ships were fairly well run, others carried their 'black ivory' in ghastly manner and many deaths occurred during a voyage through overcrowding and disease.

SLOOP OF WAR

Small, fast war vessel of the 18th and 19th centuries, used for scouting, message carrying, light engagements, etc. Early sloops were often two-masted, schooner-rigged craft, but towards the end of the 18th century many, like the example, were ship-rigged and mounted about 18 guns.

TARTANA

A small Mediterranean sailing vessel rather galley type. The example was in use during the 16th century. Her two lateen sails are fitted with brails, and increased freeboard is obtained amidships by the fitting of an extra board. Retains some semblance of the galley beak.

VIKING SHIP

These wonderful vessels, which made astounding voyages, were double-ended, and although simple in design were often of considerable size. Clincher built, they had one mast almost amidships and a square sail, but could also be propelled by oars. Steered by a special oar over the starboard quarter.

DUTCH ADMIRALTY YACHT

Admiralty yachts were attached to the Dutch fleet during the 17th and 18th centuries. They were employed as tenders, dispatch vessels, etc. Bluff bows and elaborate decorations were features of these craft. Had high stern and a beak like big ships. Mounted several small guns.

ACTUARIUS

This small vessel was employed by the Romans for the transport of supplies and other work of similar nature requiring a fast, handy ship. She was un-decked, and carried a square sail for use in favourable winds. Could also be propelled by oars. In general appearance like a very small galley.

CONVICT SHIP

A vessel used for the transport of prisoners to remote penal settlements. This example was in service at the end of the 18th century, carrying convicts to Australia. The French have a modern steamer fitted with steel cells and up-to-date methods of preventing any attempt to escape.

FISH CARRIER (Sail)

Carried salt fish from Newfoundland and Labrador to Europe. Nicknamed 'Fish Boxes.' Fast sailers, run from St. John's to Liverpool sometimes taking only 12 or 13 days. Fish in drums or bulk. When in bulk, fish had to be most carefully stowed to prevent damage from damp. Barques, brigs, schooners, etc. Varied a great deal in size.

FRUIT SCHOONER

Several hundred of these smart, fast little ships were employed in the fruit trade from the Mediterranean and Western Isles, usually discharging in the Thames or Mersey. Average dimensions were approximately 75 ft. × 20 ft. × 12 ft. depth of hold. Tonnage varied between about 100 and 160 tons.

LARGE SAILING AND AUXILIARY

LARGE SAILING AND AUXILIARY

THE sailing ship era reached its zenith with the famous tea and wool clippers, whose record passages were front page news and whose graceful lines and snowy canvas placed them among man's most beautiful creations.

But now, as a commercial proposition, wind-driven ships are dead. For some time after the advent of steam ships the clippers held their own and in many instances overtook and passed fast steamers of their day when conditions were favourable. But the power-driven ship soon established herself, giving greater regularity in service, greater average speed, increased size and consequently superior accommodation. Windships were soon relegated to the slow trades, in which duration of voyage mattered little compared with cheap freight rates.

Large European sailing vessels (mostly barque-rigged) have, of recent years, been employed only in the grain and timber trades, apart from a few smart vessels which act as ocean-going training ships.

The Americans, in a last effort to make sail pay, built multi-masted, fore-and-aft schooners, which could be handled by very small crews and were, therefore, economical to run, but even these could not make the regular profits of the steamer.

In addition to the few really big vessels still in commission, there are numerous smaller sailing craft such as coasting schooners, dhows and junks trading in various parts of the world. Yet even their numbers are rapidly diminishing, and are not being replaced.

It is ironical that the internal combustion engine, introduced long after the steam engine, should now be doing its best to keep sailing vessels at sea. Hundreds of the smaller sailers, which would long ago have been forced out of existence, have been fitted with motor engines and so just manage to pay their way.

All true ship lovers will regret the passing of sail, and future generations may never know the experience of standing on the deck of a ship heeled over by the wind, ploughing through the seas, silent but for the roar of the bow-wave and the song of the wind in her rigging.

LARGE SAILING AND AUXILIARY

AUXILIARY

A sailing vessel which is fitted with steam or motor engines for use in calms, etc. The example is a motor schooner, but auxiliaries may be of any other rig, such as barque, ketch, cutter, etc., and any type from small yachts to ocean-going vessels of 2,000 tons or more.

AUXILIARY COASTER

A common type of North European coasting vessel. Has usually a stout pole mast in tabernacle, setting main and foresail. Handy little ships, often family owned and manned, having home-like accommodation. Small enough to enter narrow rivers and little, out-of-the-way ports. Dimensions about 88 ft. × 20 ft.

BLOCK ISLAND BOAT

A small-decked sailing boat found on the east coast of America. Her hull is very similar to certain Scottish fishing craft. Has a pronounced rake to stem and stern. Two stout masts setting tall sails with short gaffs. Mainsail with boom, foresail loose-footed. Wash boards are fitted amidships.

BATEL

Open boat like small sambuk. Square stern, sloping stem. Short deck bow and stern. Some ribs extended above planking, used for making ropes fast. One mast amidships. Two shrouds each side. One of the most seaworthy of dhow family. Oiled or varnished. About 70 ft. long.

THAMES COASTING BARGE

Very strongly built ships, slightly larger than the Thames 'River' Class. Their dimensions are approximately 85 ft. × 19 ft. × 7 ft. draught loaded (17 ft. with leeboards down). Built for working all round the east and south coasts of England, also Continental ports; they are able to carry about 150 tons. Have less than 1 ft. freeboard when loaded.

PORTUGUESE CORK BARGE

The accompanying illustration shows a barge of the type used for carrying bales of natural cork down-river for export. It will be noticed that the mast is well forward, but has acute rake, bringing the mainsail far enough aft for a balanced sail-plan without reducing cargo space.

KELANI RIVER BARGE

A quaint, flat-bottomed vessel carrying local produce down-river to Colombo. Square, ark-like boats, they are heavily thatched. Drift downstream, skillfully steered by long sweeps. When empty, the craft are laboriously worked back up-river. Size varies from about 25 ft. to 60 ft. in length.

THAMES RIVER BARGE

Though similar in general lines to the coasting type, is slightly smaller. The mizen mast is smaller and farther aft, the sheet being led to the rudder blade. No bowsprit. Employed on the Thames, Medway and nearby coasts. Mast often in tabernacle. Dimensions about 80 ft. × 18 ft. × 6 ft. draught.

ST. LAWRENCE BARGE

Sometimes called 'Bateaux' and generally painted blue, the vessel illustrated appears to have something in common with the Humber Keel as regards rig, although she has a mizen mast. Employed mainly in the carriage of timber down-river to ocean-going ships for export. Length about 100 to 150 ft.

'STACKY' BARGE

This is a nickname given by the sailorman to barges loaded with hay. The cargo being of light weight is stacked to a considerable height above the deck, and a man has to be stationed on top of the 'stack' in restricted waters to direct steering as the man at the wheel cannot see ahead.

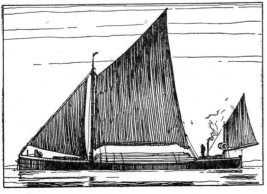

'STUMPY' BARGE

A small class of Thames and Medway sailing barge having a stout pole mast, usually in a tabernacle, but no topmast and no bowsprit. One may occasionally be seen without a mizen mast. The early ones were often swim headed. Are considered rather an inferior class of barge.

SWIM-HEADED BARGE

An early type of Thames and Medway sailing barge. Regular canvas consisted of main-sail on a sprit with brails; gaff topsail; small mizen with, in a few cases, a staysail set above tiller; foresail and jib. Cargo about 110 tons. Dimensions: 78 ft. × 17 ft. × 6 ft. draught. Sometimes set a square sail.

BARQUE

Large three-masted vessel, square-rigged on fore and main masts, fore-and-aft rigged on the mizen. The barque and four-masted barque are practically the only square-rigged vessels surviving to-day. Engaged in grain and timber trades, or used as training ships. Between about 700 and 2,000 tons.

FOUR-MASTED BARQUE

Four- or five-masted barque similar to the barque, but the extra mast or masts are square-rigged, only the aftermost one having fore-and-aft sail. Most sailing vessels in the grain trade of recent years have been of this type. Majority between about 2,000 and 3,000 tons.

BARQUENTINE

Sailing vessel rigged as follows: Three or sometimes four masts. Completely square-rigged on the foremast, fore-and-aft rigged on all others. More economical in regard to crew than completely square-rigged ships. Coasting, and some ocean-going vessels have been rigged thus, including the French ' Terre Neuva '.

JACKASS BARQUE

A rig very little used. Four masts, square-rigged fore and main masts, fore-and-aft on main and mizen. The rig was made great fun of by orthodox sailors, being likened, among other things, to 'Schooner chasing Brig'. Name 'Jackass' is sometimes applied to other freak rigs.

'BARQUE DU LEMAN'

The picturesque cargo vessel of Lake Geneva. Most northern example of lateen rig. Often sails 'Goose-winged'. Has a narrow walk-way on projecting beams along each side. Carry mostly stone. About 100 ft. × 25 ft., cargo capacity about 60 tons. Many set jib on short bowsprit.

BRAGGOZZO

A small, heavily-built, flat-bottomed fishing vessel, employed in the Adriatic. She has considerable beam and bluff bows, but is quite a fast sailer in a good breeze. As is usual with Mediterranean craft, these boats are brightly painted to the personal taste of the owner.

HERMAPHRODITE BRIG

A two-masted sailing vessel similar in size to the Brig, but instead of being square-rigged on both masts she has only fore and aft sails on the mainmast. Requires smaller crew than the full-rigged brig. Often wrongly called Brigantine. The brigantine has square topsails at the mainmast.

BUG-EYE

This vessel, in spite of her rather unpleasant name, has a graceful appearance. An American type used for coasting, etc. The tall triangular sails, with mast hoops, are very easily handled by a small crew. An interesting feature is the half-boom on the foresail. Fitted with centreplate.

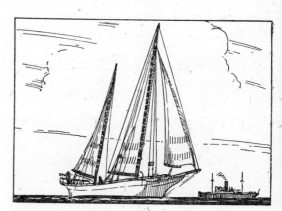

GREEK CAIQUE

Graceful cargo carriers and fast sailers. Rig varies considerably. Example has two masts with balance lug sails set on opposite sides of masts. All have a pronounced sheer. Some are now fitted with auxiliary engines. Average dimensions about 50 ft. × 10 ft. The Germans used a number of these ships during their invasion of Crete.

CHASSE MAREE

A French craft employed as a trawler and mackerel line fisherman. Three-masted vessel setting standing lugsails and square topsails. Upper topsails are sometimes set on small topmasts. The mizen mast is not often used. Manned by big crew. Heavily built to enable her to take the ground without damage.

CLIPPER

Were probably the most beautiful examples of the shipbuilders' art. With their hollow bow lines and great sail-spread, two of these vessels with the new season's tea would sometimes dock on the same tide after a race of 90 or 100 days. Sailed also with wool from Australia.

DAHABIYAH

An ancient type of Nile craft. Used by wealthy Egyptians, they were luxuriously fitted out. The modern version is steel built and fitted for travel in the greatest comfort. Although good sailers, the impatient traveller may have them towed. Approximate dimensions 110 ft. × 19 ft. Six to eight passengers.

DHANGI

An Arab trading vessel found on the west coast of India. Has a peculiar projection forward of the stem suggesting a 'beak'. Sharp sterned and a fast sailer. A capstan is mounted on the raised poop. Vary in size, the example being of about 100 tons. 75 ft. long, 22 ft. beam.

DHOW

An Arab vessel with many variations. The first-class dhow is a fine sailer, often making long voyages across Indian Ocean and down African coast. Very beamy, usually with decorated stern. One time not unconnected with slaves and piracy. Up to about 400 tons. See Pattimar, Baghla, Batel, Sambuk, etc.

EXPLORATION VESSEL

Very strongly built ship with heavy timbers, and bow strengthened and sheathed for working in ice. Such vessels were employed by Scott, Amundsen, Shackleton and others. Somewhat on lines of the old whalers. Carries large quantity of stores and fuel. Example : 179 ft. × 34 ft. × 18 ft. 6 in. 736 tons. Has auxiliary steam engine.

MERSEY FLAT

Similar to the later type of Weaver Flat, but slightly larger and with finer lines. She has a small fore hatch and main hatch divided into two by a narrow transverse space. Masts in tabernacles, although employed chiefly in the coasting trade. Dimensions were approximately 78 ft. × 21 ft. × 8 ft. 6 ins. and gross tonnage just over 100.

WEAVER FLAT

A flat-bottomed sailing barge employed on the Rivers Weaver and Mersey, chiefly in the carriage of coal and salt. This example, built early in the 19th century, had a square stern. Later were usually sharp sterned. Capacity about 60 tons on dimensions 62 ft. × 17 ft. × 6 ft. Mast in tabernacle.

HOOGARTS

Small Dutch mussel and shrimp fishing vessel, in most cases sprit rigged, and having the usual leeboards as she is a flat-bottomed craft. Features are the masthead weather vane and peculiar rudder. There is an open well with stove for boiling the catch. Belongs to the island of Walcheren.

HOOLUNG

A large type of dug-out boat used for carrying cargo and passengers on the rivers of Assam. Characteristic of this vessel are the flat 'duck bill' ends, sometimes decorated with carving. Propelled by oars, or by long poles in shallow water. Has two shelters to protect passengers and cargo.

JAEGT

An ancient type of Norwegian coaster still employed carrying dried fish, etc. Square sail and high ends are reminiscent of the early Norsemen. The mainsail is fitted with a bonnet, and a square topsail is sometimes set. Occasionally chartered for wedding parties, etc. when she is elaborately decorated.

BURMESE JUNK

Passenger and cargo vessel of the Irrawadi, used chiefly for carriage of rice. The ladder mast and many lifts led aft are reminiscent of ancient Egyptian ships. Sail is set on rings like a curtain. Hull is dug out of large tree and built up with planks. Local name, 'Laungzat'.

ICHANG RIVER JUNK

A shallow draught vessel designed for working on the upper reaches of the Yangtze. A deck-house provides shelter for the helmsman, and a pair of long oars called 'yulows' are carried. The main and mizen masts are almost vertical, while the foremast has a pronounced forward rake.

JAPANESE JUNK

Unlike Chinese junks, the example has no battens on the sails. The seams are roped to take weight of sail. Open stern, steered by a long tiller with tackles. The narrow, bound tassel at her bow denotes that she is a trading vessel. The two little sails forward assist steering.

MANDARIN JUNK

A Chinese ceremonial vessel reserved for the use of high personages. The accommodation is beautifully built and elaborately ornamented. The masts are placed well forward and the stern is adorned with numerous flags. She is a shallow draught ship carrying a number of sweeps for use in calms.

PEKING RIVER JUNK

This craft is a shallow water type, beamy, flat-bottomed, with more elaborate deck erections than the Ichang example. Also has only one mast. Steering is assisted, when shooting rapids, by a man in the bows with a long sweep. Draws only a foot or so of water.

SHANTUNG JUNK

Trades between Yellow Sea ports and down to Shanghai. The hull is whale-backed, somewhat like the Western 'Turret-deck' steamer. Has five masts, three on the centre line, and two smaller ones on the extreme port side. Sails are of tanned canvas. Dimensions about 150 ft. × 32 ft.

SWATOW FISHING JUNK

A sea-going trawler from the Formosa Channel. She is a good heavy weather boat, with a broad stern recessed to take the long rudder which extends far below the keel and is fitted with raising tackle. The nets are towed between two boats. Approximate dimensions : 50 ft. × 14 ft.

HUMBER KEEL

Flat-bottomed Yorkshire vessel carrying about 100 tons. Big hatch occupies nearly all deck space. Mast is in tabernacle, all running rigging of wire, worked by hand winches. The stern rails are supported on extended timbers. Leeboards are worked from aft. Dimensions about 60 ft. × 15 ft. Draught 7 ft.

KETCH

At first sight very similar to the yawl, but it will be noticed that her mizen mast is larger and stepped forward of the rudder post. A popular rig among sailing trawlers and yachts. Most fishing vessels of Brixham and Lowestoft, also certain barges and coasters are of this rig.

BALTIC KETCH

Wooden built coasting vessel of the Baltic with an unusual rig. Although, to all intents and purposes a ketch, she crosses yards and sets square sails on the main mast. Also on this mast is set a very square fore-and-aft topsail rather similar to that of the Tasmanian Ketch.

COASTING KETCH

Small ketch-rigged trading vessel, once popular for coasting work and still to be seen chiefly in West of England. The majority have now been fitted with auxiliary power. Their most usual cargoes are coal, china clay and bricks. In size they vary between about 50 and 80 tons.

TASMANIAN KETCH

Their large square topsails give these coasters a distinctive appearance. Some are now fitted with auxiliary engines. Range between about 10 and 90 tons. At present about 40 boats are registered at Hobart, and 15 at Launceston. Carry mostly stores to outlying coastal districts, returning with farm produce, timber, etc.

KLIPPER

Dutch, iron-built, sailing cargo vessel, generally ketch-rigged. Mast in tabernacle for lowering. Has a huge horizontal steering-wheel which facilitates manœuvring in narrow waterways. Practically the whole of the hull interior is occupied by cargo space.

LAKATOI

A native of New Guinea, this quaint craft is built of two dugout canoes with a platform over. The boats are about 35 ft. long and about 5 ft. apart. The peculiar crab-claw sail is made of matting strips. Upwards of thirty people can be carried on such ships.

LORCHA

An eastern trading vessel with European type hull, but Chinese rig for simple handling by native crews. Employed in the early 19th century by European companies, often in the opium trade. Fast sailer, lug-rigged with battens to keep sails flat when beating to windward. Sails are of canvas.

CORNISH LUGGER

Boat used largely for pilchard fishing. Sets a dipping lugsail on mainmast, standing lug on mizen. Dipping lugs must be lowered and set again on the other side of mast when tacking. Boat has long outrigger at stern to which mizen sheet is led. About 47 ft. × 13 ft. 6 ins. × 7 ft. draught.

MAHAILA

Largest type of native vessel plying on the river between Baghdad and Basrah. She has a mast with forward rake and is lateen-rigged. The heavy rudder has great fore-and-aft length, but is scarcely a couple of feet in depth. A feature of these boats is their pronounced sheer.

MARAJO FISHING BOAT

These rakish little craft are employed in fishing the channels of the Amazon mouth and nearby coasts. They come from the Island of Marajo at the entrance to the great river. About 40 ft. in length with distinctive appearance by reason of the raked mast and extremely long boom.

PATTIMAR

Numerous coasting vessels on Indian coast between Colombo and Bombay. Pronounced sheer. Usually painted red and black. Masts raked forward. Sometimes small temporary mast at stern. Have a thatched shelter erection on deck between the masts. Semi-open boats. Carry a jib boom. About 100 ft. in length.

BESUKI PRAHU

Largest type of Javanese fishing vessel, with approximate dimensions 42 ft. × 10 ft. 6 ins. She uses a kind of seine net, and usually carries a small boat to assist in manipulating this. A crew of twenty or more is carried as propulsion by oars is sometimes necessary. Steered by an attached paddle.

PROW

Cargo carrier, undecked except for a small section amidships where crew sleep and live. Employed in Bombay Harbour. She has very long, straight stem with pronounced rake. Fine lines forward, heavy aft. Round stern. Steering is by tiller. Having small sail area is slow sailer. Largest about 100 tons.

SAMBUK

A member of the dhow family carrying passengers. Faster, but smaller than the 'Baghla'. Little sheer. Hull roughly built, square stern, no ornamentation. Completely decked and has two masts. An iron tiller is fitted with lines to a wheel. Typical dimensions : 64 ft. × 18 ft. × 10 ft. 6 ins.

SCHOKKER

A Dutch craft of characteristically stout construction. Her straight, acutely-raked stem is particularly heavy, and is divided at the head to take the peculiar grapnel anchor. She has narrow leeboards, and a short curved gaff on the mainsail, which is laced to the mast but not to the boom.

FORE-AND-AFT SCHOONER

An economical rig which can be worked by a small crew. The rig has been used on various types of vessel—yachts, coasters, ocean-going merchant ships, etc. Usually two- or three-masted, but American schooners have been built with as many as seven. (See American schooner and Great Lakes schooner.)

AMERICAN SCHOONER

With beauty sacrificed to efficiency, the steel-hulled, multi-masted American trading schooner is a determined effort to make wind ships pay their way under modern conditions. The fore-and-aft rig, with deck winches for running gear, is handled by small crews. Built up to about 5,000 tons.

GREAT LAKES SCHOONER

These vessels were employed in the lumber grain, ore and coal trade of the Lakes. Varied in detail according to service. Two-, three- or four-masted. Interesting feature of rig is the triangular 'raffee' topsail on the foremast. Some of smaller class fitted with centre-plates. Example about 260 tons.

GRAND BANKS SCHOONER

Strong, fast, yacht-like vessels, rigged as two-masted schooners. Employed on Newfoundland Banks cod fishing. Fishing is done with lines from dories which are stowed on deck. Work from Nova Scotia and Gloucester, Mass. Great rivalry exists between the two places. About 35 tons.

STAYSAIL SCHOONER

Chiefly a rig favoured by large yachts. She is a two-masted vessel. Instead of the usual Bermudian or gaff sail on the foremast, a large staysail is set on the mainstay, between the two masts. The example has booms on staysails as well as on the Bermudian mainsail.

TOPSAIL SCHOONER

A type of sailing vessel which was at one time very popular in the British coasting trade, but now almost extinct. Distinguished from the fore-and-aft schooner by yards crossed on the foremast for square topsails. Dimensions approximately as follows: 100 ft. × 24 ft., 100 to 150 tons.

NEW ZEALAND SCOW

A coasting vessel varying in size from about 25 to 200 tons. Employed in the carriage of timber, coal, grain, case oil, etc. Built of wood, the majority now have auxiliary power. One of average size—say 80 tons—carries a crew of six. Square stern is a feature.

FULL-RIGGED SHIP

A large three-masted vessel having the masts each in three sections—lower-mast, topmast and topgallant-mast. She is completely square-rigged on all masts. Although very popular at the height of the clipper ship era, needed big crews, and were later largely replaced by barques.

SNOW

There is little to distinguish the Snow from a brig, their general lines and rig being identical, except that the Snow has a light trysail mast just abaft the main lower mast. This arrangement allows a fore-and-aft sail with mast-hoops, also square course to be set on the mainmast.

SUKUNG

Javanese fishing boat with outriggers, a peculiarity being that the after supports of these are curved upwards. The triangular sail is somewhat like that of the Fiji boats. Her rudder is carried over the side in the manner of a steering-oar. The lower end of the yard rests in a socket.

'TERRE NEUVA'

A fast-disappearing type of sailing vessel which crosses to the Grand Banks from St. Malo and Fécamp. Stout ships—usually barquentine-rigged—carrying about a dozen dories stowed on deck. In size these vessels may reach about 1,000 tons, and are manned by a crew of about fifty men.

TJALK

Dutch sailing vessel with round, apple bow and stern. Flat-bottomed. The mast can be lowered and the sail has a short, straight gaff. Vary in size, the large ones, as shown, having high sterns and pronounced sheer. The smaller class have a curved gaff and much less sheer.

CONCARNEAU TUNNY BOAT

Yawl-rigged boat between 50 and 90 tons, used for deep-sea tunny fishing. At sea about a fortnight. Long rods are rigged each side, from which trail several lines. Fine, stout sea boat, painted in brilliant colours. Rods are stowed against the mast when not in use.

ULAK

A Bengalese produce barge, the Ulak is a beamy, double-ended craft, with a square sail plan rather like that of the Humber Keel. There is a short deck at bow and stern, the midship part being open but covered by a thatch roof as protection for the cargo. 38 ft. × 14 ft.

NEW BEDFORD WHALER

Employed in Arctic whaling during 19th and early 20th century. Most usual type were barques—sometimes with auxiliary steam power—of about 500 tons. Hull sheathed with greenheart wood to withstand ice wear. Carried six whaleboats on stout wooden davits. Had stove and boiler on deck for treating blubber.

NORFOLK WHERRY

A cargo vessel of the Norfolk Broads. Clinker built, almost double-ended, a false keel is bolted on to assist sailing. The heavy mast, weighted at the heel, is in a tabernacle. It is traditional to have a white painted semi-circle on the bows. Dimensions about 55 ft. × 16 ft. 6 ins.

WISHBONE-RIGGED VESSEL

Unorthodox yacht rig tried fairly extensively in United States and elsewhere. The mainsail, in one piece from foot to masthead, is extended between a kind of double gaff, more or less wishbone shape, which is sheeted to the mizen mast. May be used on ketch or schooner.

CRUISING YACHT

A yacht of any size from about 20 ft. in length upwards, built for cruising as distinct from racing. Has sleeping accommodation, cooking apparatus, etc. A beamier boat with fuller lines than the racer. Majority have auxiliary power. Usually sloop, cutter, yawl or ketch rig. The 'Ocean Racer' combines cruising and racing.

'J' CLASS YACHT

This is the largest class of racing yacht. In length they vary between about 100 and 130 ft. with sail area around 7,500 sq. ft. The Bermudian-rigged mast is about 160 ft. in height. These are the wonderful racing machines which competed for the America Cup, crossing the Atlantic under special rig.

30 SQUARE METRE YACHT

A modern racer, about half the size of the 12-metre, or a little longer and beamier than the 6-metre, but with less draught and short keel. Sail plan is narrow, both the end of the boom and tack of headsails being well inboard. The design originated in the Baltic.

TWELVE-METRE YACHT

One of the most popular classes among larger racing yachts. Although originally of 12 metres (about 39 ft. 5 ins.) waterline length, sail area, 2,600 sq. ft., the modern boats are 45 to 46 ft. with sail area 1,900 sq. ft., 9 ft. draught. Majority of masts are hollow wood but metal is allowed.

ZULU

Scottish fishing lugger with a 'Fifie' bow, but the raked stern of a 'Skaffie'. This craft very largely replaced the 'Skaffie'. The example has wheel steering. She is a decked boat with dimensions about 54 ft. × 16 ft. 6 ins. The type has, in the last few years, become practically extinct.

BAGHLA

Largest member of dhow family. Long, sloping bow with extended and ornamented stem. Square stern, carved. Hull either varnished or treated with oil. Steered by wheel. Completely decked. Third small mast sometimes stepped right aft with lateen sail in fair weather. Main yard about length of ship. Tonnage about 400.

GYASSA

A large Nile cargo vessel. The tall lateen sails are used for running up-river before the prevailing wind, while the return is usually a drift with the current. An interesting feature is the bluff, turned-up bow, which will not stick in if the craft rams the high, soft river banks.

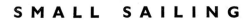

SMALL SAILING

SMALL SAILING

THE majority of vessels in this section are native craft and fishermen. Among them, perhaps more than in any other section, may be seen a fine balance of craftsmanship and ingenuity in the adaptation of each vessel to its own particular local conditions. Thus, in shallow waters where deep-keel boats would be impracticable, we find light-draught hulls, many with false keels which may be raised or lowered at will, and modifications of the 'barge' carrying lee-boards.

In competent hands there is almost no limit to the length of voyages which can be undertaken by small ships. This has been demonstrated time and again by lone world-voyagers and Pacific Island natives. These natives have made astonishing ocean crossings in their frail-looking out-riggers, although, it must be admitted, such voyages were sometimes the result of accident rather than design, the unfortunate vessel being swept to leeward of her destination by some trick of the wind or current.

Here also are the craft of the man who ' carries his boat on his back.' Canoes, coracles, mussucks, are all capable of being lifted from the water by one man and carried overland without difficulty. Mussucks might possibly be described as the earliest form of collapsible boat, although ' deflatable ' would be a more accurate description.

SMALL SAILING

BAIDARKA

Boat belonging to the Eskimos of Northern Alaska. It is framed in driftwood and the covering is of sealskin. Differs from the one-man, sharp-ended Greenland kayak in holding two men and having a rather blunt bow with a hole in it for attaching a rope. Dimensions : 14 ft. × 2 ft.

'BALDIE'

A small lug-rigged open boat from the east coast of Scotland, used by inshore fishermen. Very strongly built with heavy timbers and a deep, straight keel. Similar in some respects to the much larger 'Fifie', but has a certain amount of rake on the stem and stern posts.

BALSA

A boat made from the extraordinarily light Balsa wood and coarse grass. Used on Lake Titicaca. Has a small sail of grass. The craft is steered by an oar over the side, moved in the desired direction by the man's leg and foot.

D

BANCA

A sailing boat of the outrigger type, whose home is in the Philippine Islands. Employed by natives of the Moro tribe in pearling, etc. The rectangular sail is set on a tripod mast, and the boat is a fast sailer. Large tassels and patches of colour decorate the sail.

CANADIAN BATEAU

A double-ended, flat-bottomed boat used extensively for various purposes in the United States and Canada. Measurements, anything from about 12 to 80 ft. in length. The small boats are usually paddled, the larger ones rowed and steered with a paddle. Similar in many respects to the Dory.

BAWLEY

A Thames Estuary fishing vessel for shrimps and whitebait, conspicuous for her long top-mast. The mainsail is set loose-footed on a long gaff, and may be brailed up. Has wide, square stern. Now much reduced in numbers and fitted with engines. Approximate length, 35 ft. Sail area about 970 sq. ft.

BELLUM ASHARI

A lean, shallow boat, sharp at bow and stern. The ends curve sharply upwards and are ornamented. All these craft are painted white. They traverse the waterways around Basrah, propelled by two men wielding poles or paddles according to the depth of water.

BERMUDA BOAT

The boat from which sprang the modern Bermudian rig. Characteristics are the long mast, to which the head of the sail is usually 'lashed'. Long boom extending forward of the mast, and hauled aft with a tackle to stretch the foot of the sail. About 25 ft. × 7 ft. Mast 44 ft.

TURKISH CAIQUE

A narrow open boat whose home is the Bosphorus. In some cases she has a light fancy awning at the stern, and is elaborately ornamented as example. The oars have heavy, egg-shaped thicknesses of wood near inboard ends as balance against that part of the oar outside the boat.

CHINESE 'AUTOMATIC' FISHING CANOE

Canoe with white board or canvas sloping into water. Net is slung along opposite side. Bamboo bow makes rattling noise. Used at night with a lamp. When fish hear the rattle and swim over white board, they become frightened and leap into the boat or the net.

BIRCH BARK CANOE

Built of pieces of bark on a light wooden framework, fastenings usually being of pliable tree roots. Seams made tight with resin. Able to face rough water, yet light enough to be carried long distances overland, as they often have to be past rapids, etc. Used by Red Indians originally.

CANVAS CANOE

Although these canoes vary somewhat in design and size, the one illustrated, 10 ft. 6 ins. × 30 ins. × 12 ins. depth amidships will give a fair idea of their appearance and construction. The narrow stringers and ribs of wood are covered with painted canvas, the whole forming a light, strong craft.

FIJI CANOE

Narrow dug-out craft of outrigger type. Having only one outrigger, and that always being kept on the windward side when sailing, the boat is double-ended and may be sailed either way. Mast is pivoted and rake is reversed when going about. The light sail is of matting.

INFLATED CANOE

A collapsible craft made of waterproofed cotton fabric and inflated with air. The example, 14 ft. in length, has several air compartments and will carry three persons. It weighs 35 lbs. Specially convenient for touring, camping, etc. Propelled by paddles. Extremely buoyant.

INTERNATIONAL CANOE

Between 16 and 17 ft. in length; beam about 3 ft. 6 ins. Raced under Royal Canoe Club and American Canoe Association rules. Has a self-draining cockpit and sliding seat for helmsman. A centre plate is fitted. Very fast and, being quite watertight, may be sailed in open water.

ROB ROY CANOE

A graceful, smartly-finished craft with dimensions approximately 12 ft. 6 ins. × 2 ft. 2 ins. × 9 ins. depth amidships. Built of planks only about $\frac{3}{16}$ in. thick, the weight is around 50-60 pounds. Sometimes fitted with a light mast and lugsail. Completely decked with the exception of a small opening amidships.

CATBOAT

The 'Cat' or 'Una' boat originated in America. Beamy and flat-bottomed with centre-board. The mast is right forward and the one large sail has a gaff and boom. Not much of a sea boat, but very fast and handy in shallow waters, drawing only a few inches with the plate up.

CATAMARAN

A small, raft-like structure consisting of several logs lashed together. On the Indian coast were of great service before the days of artificial harbours for taking messages to ships lying off shore. The name is often wrongly applied to various outrigger canoes, etc.

CAYUKA

A large, heavy type of dug-out boat employed by the Panama Indians for the transport of fruit—mostly bananas—and other native produce. Roughly hewn out of hard wood, the craft has quite a large carrying capacity. Propelled by paddles or poles. Dimensions about 20 ft. × 4 ft. 6 ins.

CHINEDKULAN

A native boat from the little island of Kota-sho just south of Formosa. She is beautifully and elaborately ornamented according to certain traditional designs, the pattern being worked in lime and soot. Propelled by rowing, the crew consisting of ten oarsmen and one with a long steering-paddle.

COBLE

Open fishing, lug-rigged boat of Northumberland and Yorkshire. Has deep forefoot, running up to a flat bottom aft where stout bilge keels are fitted. Narrow rudder extends below stern. Fine sea boat, particularly suitable for beaching. This is done by unshipping the rudder and running in under oars, stern first.

COCKLER

Small, centre-board craft, now all fitted with engines, employed in cockle fishing in Thames Estuary. The mainsail is set loose-footed on a long gaff similar to that of the Bawley. No topmast. The hull is divided into cabin, hold and machinery space. Length about 35 ft.

CORACLE

There are still a number of these primitive craft in the remote parts of Ireland and Wales. They consist of a framework of ash or willow, Sometimes re-inforced with basket work, and covered with tarred canvas or sewn skin. sufficiently light to be carried easily on a man's back.

CURRAGH

Primitive Irish craft still used in remote parts. Have wood or wicker covered with tarred canvas. Some are propelled by oars which have lugs to fit on to single thole pins. Vary considerably. The example is used for crossing between Aran Islands and mainland. Sizes from about 9 ft. to 16 ft.

CUTTER-RIGGED VESSEL

Originally any small craft having one mast and a bowsprit which could be run in along the deck, and setting mainsail, gaff-topsail, fore-sail and one or more jibs. Modern Bermudian-rigged racing yachts are considered to be cutters, having two or more headsails but no bowsprit.

PILOT CUTTER (Sail)

These sturdy little ships have been super-ceded by steam or motor cutters, but they are wonderful vessels for keeping the sea in all weathers, and a great many have been bought for conversion into yachts, particularly those from the Bristol Channel. They are probably the best known British type.

14 ft. INTERNATIONAL DINGHY

A beautiful little racer, very popular in sheltered waters. Although so small many first-class boats cost around £150 with fittings and hollow mast which may be 25 ft. in height. Bermudian-rigged and fitted with centre-plate. Draught about 9 ins. (5 ft. with plate down).

DORY

A flat-bottomed open boat carried by Grand Banks fishing vessels. Several boats spread out around the parent ship and fishing is done with lines. A number are stowed in limited space by placing one inside another. Double-ended but for a narrow V-shaped transom. Length about 15 ft.

FELUCCA

A Spanish and Portuguese type of sailing vessel employed in various coasting trades. She is a very fast sailer, both running and when beating to windward. When going about the shrouds are alternately slacked away to allow play for the yards. Now often lug-rigged. Example 40 ft. × 11 ft.

FERILLA

A gaily-painted Maltese boat which still shows traces of the ancient galley beak. A tiny triangular sail is set on a boom similar to that of the modern spinnaker. It will be noticed that the heel of the slender sprit is some distance from the mast.

' FIFIE '

A type of Scottish fishing boat. In many ways similar to the 'Skaffie', but has straight, vertical stem and stern posts. Originally open boats, they were first decked about middle 19th century. There is a strong likeness between these craft and the Cornish lugger. Now usually fitted with engines.

WARSHIP'S GALLEY

A rowing and sailing boat carried by large warships. The gig is a similar boat but slightly smaller. Area of Galley's mainsail is about 150 sq. ft., mizen 120 sq. ft. dipping lugs. Life-saving capacity twenty-eight persons in reasonable weather. Her dimensions are as follows : 32 ft. × 5 ft. 11 ins.

GONDOLA

A flat-bottomed boat employed in passenger-carrying on the waterways of Venice. Is peculiar in being built with its two sides unequal. This gives the boat a list which is rectified when the oarsman takes up his position. Some examples belonging to wealthy owners are most luxuriously appointed.

GUFA

Mesopotamian craft built of wickerwork covered with skins and made watertight with pitch. They are perfectly round, and sometimes of considerable size, being able to carry sheep and even horses across wide rivers. Very similar in construction to the coracle. Usually propelled by paddles or a long pole.

GUNDALOW

A queer type of barge, now obsolete, which sailed the Merrimac River in New Hampshire. The rig is very un-American, consisting of a 'balanced lateen' heavily weighted at the lower end, so that the yard may be easily raised or lowered. The sail is fitted with brails.

GALWAY HOOKER

West of Ireland craft, carrying turf, etc. These little cutter-rigged boats have a short deck forward but are otherwise open. The hull has considerable tumble-home aft, and is fitted with wash strakes. The sails are treated with tar and grease. Crew of two. Dimensions about 35 ft. × 11 ft. × 6 ft. draught aft.

HODY

A double-ended, undecked, Bombay fishing boat. Has a curved stem, straight stern post and little sheer. Wash boards are fitted forward of amidships. There are thole pins in the gunwale for oars. Crew of a dozen or so for working nets. Length approximately 25-40 ft.

HURJIA

An extremely ancient type of boat from the Persian Gulf. The hull is constructed of palm leaf stems, and has a double bottom. Is not caulked, so water comes up to the inner floor when carrying a load. Has a light mast amidships with the usual lateen sail.

KARACHI JOLLY BOAT

A small, open, lateen-rigged craft used for passenger-carrying in Bombay Harbour. The Mast is lashed to a thwartship beam, and is supported by one shroud each side. Good sea boat. Usually painted in bright colours, and displays a plimsol mark. Awning often rigged over passengers. About 9 tons register.

KOLEH

A native craft of the Straights Settlements used for fishing. Long and narrow, sprit-rigged with a jib, and occasionally seen with a small mizen. A number of these boats used to be raced at Singapore, when they would carry a crew of about fourteen men. About 30 ft. in length.

KOSTER

Named after the Island of Koster, on the west coast of Sweden. Were often used by smugglers in years gone by, and later as a fishing boat or yacht. Clincher built. Length about 20-35 ft. The type is a very good sea boat in skilful hands. Has a fore hatch, large well amidships and small square cockpit aft.

LAKE DAL FISHING BOAT

The hull, built of three wide planks of pine, has a sharp bow and a small platform at the stern. The side planks are secured to the bottom with iron spikes. Propelled by a carved wooden paddle. Fishing is done with a light, seven-pronged spear about 15 ft. long.

CHINESE RIVER LIFEBOAT

Called locally ' Red Boats ' (they are painted bright red) these stoutly-built lifeboats are stationed on the upper Yangtse River. Kept in readiness to assist vessels in distress on the rapids. The steering-oar is about one and a half times the length of the boat. Dimensions about 35 ft. × 7 ft. 6 ins.

PULLING AND SAILING LIFEBOAT

Operated by the Royal National Lifeboat Institution, a diagonally-planked boat fitted with buoyancy tanks. The example is self-righting—see high air cases at bow and stern. Valves are fitted, automatically draining the boat of water. Dimensions about 33 ft. × 8 ft. Now almost entirely replaced by motor boats.

SHIP'S LIFEBOAT

A double-ended open boat of at least 125 cubic feet capacity, fitted with buoyancy tanks. May be either clincher, diagonal or steel built. Mast and sails are included in the equipment. Several epic voyages of thousands of miles have been made in ships' boats.

HASTINGS LUGGER

This was a beamy, lute-sterned boat, the illustration showing one of about 1890. The masts are in tabernacles, a dipping lug being set on the main and standing lug on the mizen. A powerful, decked craft working from the open beach. Present-day boats have engines. Dimensions : 28 ft. × 11 ft.

GRAVELINES LUGGER

This old-fashioned type of French fishing vessel is a stout craft, straight sided with heavy transom. The lug sails are cut particularly square. She is an exceptionally small ship to be fitted with three masts. Gradually being replaced by ketch-rigged boats. Length somewhere around 60 ft.

FLUSHING PILOT LUGGER

A long, open boat, rigged with main-mast amidships and a small mizen-mast at the extreme stern with outrigger to extend the sheet. Somewhat similar to early luggers of the English South coast. She is used to take pilots to and from vessels navigating the Schelde.

MALDIVE ISLAND FISHING BOAT

Strong, shallow-draught boat employed for catching bonito. Has a wide platform at the stern and is divided into several compartments. The mast is stepped in a tabernacle. Sets a tall, square sail, and a fore-and-aft sail on a gaff, but loose-footed.

MASHUF

A light boat built of thin wood and reeds. It is used as a vehicle by the inhabitants of a district of creeks and swamps in the vicinity of Basrah. Here the waterways are almost as much 'streets' as those of Venice. The Mashuf is of very ancient origin.

MASULA

A Madras surf boat used for lighterage service between the beach and ships at anchor, before the port had a harbour. Flat-bottomed, having wide planks sewn together with fibre. She is slightly flexible and this saves her from damage in the heavy breakers. Propelled by spear-shaped paddles.

MASHUA

Arab ship's boat. Heavily built of rough-hewn timber. The topsides are usually black or oiled, the bottom whitened with concoction of vegetable oil and lime. Has six oars and a lateen sail can be set on the stout forward-raked mast when conditions are favourable. Length about 15 ft.

'MULE'

A type of coble built at Scarborough and Filey. Her chief difference from the ordinary coble is that she has a sharp stern. This fine after end makes the 'mule' much easier to handle in a heavy following sea. Many of these boats are now fitted with motor engines.

MULETTA

A Portuguese trawler from the Tagus. Has a peculiar, almost concave bottom which allows the boat to remain upright when beached. Assortment of sails, chiefly to regulate her speed when trawling. Her length is about 50 ft., and a crew of fifteen to eighteen men is carried.

'MUMBLE BEE'

A small type of Brixham fishing vessel using a beam trawl. She is about 35-40 ft. in length, cutter-rigged with very large foresail. The beam of trawl is about 35 ft. long, made up of two sections. Fish, when caught, are sorted: large into boxes, smaller ones into baskets.

MUSSUCK

A weird-looking but useful contrivance used by natives of India for crossing rivers. It is simply an inflated skin. The man either sits astride and propels it with a paddle, or lies on the craft and kicks. Inflated by the native's mouth through one of the animal's legs.

PETER-BOAT

A small Thames fishing vessel of the 18th and early 19th centuries. She was fitted with a wet well amidships for carrying the catch, and sometimes had a removable cabin top. Spritsail rig. Double-ended, clincher built. worked up as far as London Bridge. Example: 19 ft. × 7 ft.

POOKHAUN

A little Irish fisherman and turf-carrier still using sail exclusively. Native of the west coast similar to the Hooker, but smaller and lug-rigged. Has a stout mast unsupported by shrouds, and is undecked. Worked by a crew of two. Approximate dimensions are 28 ft. × 8 ft. × 3 ft. draught.

AMERICAN SHOOTING PUNT

A portable craft, diagonally framed, and is so constructed that, by the use of wing nuts and hinges, it can be folded flat for carrying. The frame is covered with waterproof canvas. Size is about 14 ft. × 3 ft. × 1 ft. Being employed on marshes and shallow creeks they are usually poled.

FISHING PUNT

A strongly-built boat, usually of pine or spruce, with dimensions about 18 ft. × 4 ft. × 13 ins. There is a small flooded compartment amidships, extending across the punt for the storage of live bait. This has small holes along the sides for the circulation of river water. Propelled by a light pole.

GUN PUNT

Used for stalking wild fowl in shallow creeks, etc. Flat-bottomed with raked ends. A cambered deck keeps her dry in rough water. Propelled by sticks or paddles. The large gun points forward on a rest. The occupant lies in the well when stalking. Length about 18 ft.

QUAY PUNT

Originally built as tenders to sailing ships lying in Falmouth Bay. Good sea boats, deep draught. Can be sailed single-handed. A lug-sail was sometimes set instead of the 'leg of mutton' mizen. Short mast to avoid fouling ship's rigging. Decked at bow and sides. Approximate dimensions 26 ft. × 8 ft.

BARGE YACHT

Type of boat particularly suited to districts where there are extensive sandbanks, shallow creeks, etc. Built on the lines of a Thames barge, with leeboards, she will lie upright when aground. Usually yawl-rigged, with gaff and boom instead of a sprit. The example is about 35 ft. in length.

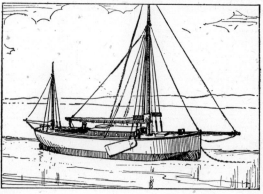

RANGOON SAMPAN

Employed on passenger and general services in Rangoon Harbour, this graceful craft is of considerably lighter construction than the ordinary Chinese Sampan, and the upward curve is much more pronounced. The sheer strake is often elaborately ornamented. The oarsman stands near the open crescent stern, facing forward.

BILGEBOARD SCOW

Light racing boat of 'skimming dish' type, 20 to 25 ft. long. Popular in S. Africa, United States and Canada. Has twin rudders and dropping bilge plates set outwards at an angle, so that when heeling the lee plate is vertical. Large sail area. Carries a crew of three or four.

SHARPIE

A handy, shallow-draught boat suitable for river or short sea sailing. Hard chine, centreboard craft setting main and foresail. For sleeping aboard, a light cover may be stretched over the boom and fastened to the edges of the cockpit. Dimensions about 14 ft. × 4 ft. 6 ins.

'SKAFFIE'

A two-masted Scottish fishing lugger, probably developed from the Yole. She has acutely-raked stem and stern posts, is completely decked with a large hatch amidships. Since the beginning of the present century their place has been largely taken by the Zulu, a sharp-sterned coble.

E

COLCHESTER SMACK

Small English East coast oyster fisherman sailing out of Colchester and Brightlingsea. Has a flat, short counter over which the oyster dredge is hauled. Some have high companionway with sliding hatch. Practically all now have auxiliary engines. Length about 32-45 ft. Older boats often had 'channels' for shrouds.

WHITSTABLE OYSTER SMACK

Cutter-rigged boat with squarish topsail. Has a broad stern like the Colchester smack, but with heavier counter. Carries a crew of three or four men, each working several 'dredges' as the oyster nets are called. Boats are 40 to 50 ft. in length. Now fitted with motor engines.

TOSHER

Small Cornish motor fishing boat, open except for a short deck forward. Carvel built. She has a stout pole mast with small, loose-footed sail on a gaff used chiefly for steadying. Employed mostly for mackerel line fishing, the boats working in wide circles. About 20 to 23 ft. in length.

TRISTAN DA CUNHA BOAT

The inhabitants of this little colony have built a number of fine boats for their purpose. Stem, stern and keel are constructed from the remains of wrecks, the timbers and knees from bent wild-apple boughs which grow on the Island. The framework is covered with canvas. Dimensions about 30 ft. × 5 ft.

UMYAK

An Eskimo boat, much larger than the Bai-darka or kayak, used for transporting whole families and goods. Built of wood lashed together and covered with skins. The largest boats are about 40 ft. long. Sometimes set a square sail in following winds. The name Umyak means ' Women's Boat.'

WHALE BOAT

Strong, fast-sailing boat carried by old whaling ships, and used in harpooning. Double-ended with centreplate. Mast in tabernacle. Fitted with rudder but often steered by an oar. Two tubs hold harpoon line, and a roller chock at stem allows line to run out freely. About 28-30 ft. in length.

WARSHIP'S WHALER

Open rowing and sailing boat with curved stem and stern posts. Built in two sizes: 25 ft. and 27 ft. in length, 6 ft. beam. The mainmast, in a clamp against the second thwart, carries a foresail and lug mainsail. Mizen has leg-of-mutton sail. A drop keel is fitted, and a movable towing bollard.

LJUNGSTRÖM-RIGGED YACHT

Invented by Dr. Ljungström of Sweden. Heavy mast stepped forward with single stay to end of counter. Mast rotated to suit angle of sail, also to reef. Battens being vertical, sail can be completely furled round the mast.

YAWL

Mainly a yacht rig. The yawl, like the ketch, has two masts, but the mizen is smaller in proportion and is stepped aft of the rudder post. The mizen sheet is led to a bumpkin extending from the stern. Thames barge has her mizen sheeted to top of rudder blade.

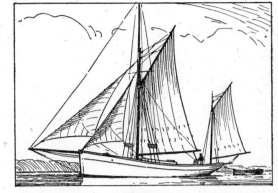

YOLE

A small, open, Shetland fishing boat of Viking origin. She still retains the Viking feature of having her ribs joined to the keel by the garboard strake of planking only. A beamy craft with fine lines at bow and stern. The mast is amidships and practically vertical.

PRAM

A type of dinghy having a flat, cut off bow instead of a sharp stem. Although difficult against a head sea, she has the advantages of being cheap to build, carrying more weight for her length than the normal dinghy, and being handy to stow in small space. Of Norwegian origin.

TANKWA

A canoe from Lake Tana, somewhat similar to the 'Hurjia' and the 'Balsa'. Built of papyrus reed stems. Size varies considerably, large boats being able to carry up to about 3 tons. Propelled by poles used like paddles at bow and stern. Must be dried out frequently, and may only last a few weeks.

MERCHANT SHIPS

MERCHANT SHIPS

THE design and construction of merchant ships have made considerable progress during the last few years and still further efforts are constantly being made to improve ships by theoretical calculation, model experiments in the testing tank, and the trial of various features in actual vessels under sea conditions. In this age of specialisation every ship is designed for her own particular service, great care being taken to give her the maximum cargo or passenger capacity that is consistent with safety and dependability, speed combined with economy, and all the other qualities essential to efficient and profitable service.

Even the humble tramp steamer is now built for efficiency; economy in initial outlay being a secondary consideration.

Since Parsons invented the turbine several new kinds of propelling machinery have been widely adopted. Motorships are becoming ever more numerous; electric power from dynamos, driven either by diesel or steam turbine engines, is used to propel a great many vessels. The Voith-Schneider combined propelling and steering unit controlled from the bridge has been successfully installed in a wide variety of ships.

Other modern features are the round 'stem' of curved plating, the Maierform bow, streamlined superstructure and steel hatch covers, also the increased use of motor lifeboats on large liners.

MERCHANT SHIPS

ARCFORM SHIP

A ship built to the special hull design of this name invented by Sir Joseph Isherwood, claimed to give improved service and economy in fuel. In midship section the ship has convex sides instead of the usual flat walls. The first of this type was a 4,000-ton ship completed in 1933.

ARCH FRAME VESSEL

A system of construction in which the upper ends of the side frames are curved sharply inwards to the deck beams. The ship also has a slightly inverse sheer. These two features combined allow large clear holds owing to increased strength. A number of colliers have been built on this principle.

MOTOR CANAL BARGE

These craft, called 'narrow boats', have replaced the horse-drawn narrow boat on many English canals. The hull is about 70 ft. long with beam of 7 ft. divided into fore peak, cargo hold, living accommodation, and engine space. Draught limited to 3ft. 6ins. Engine 15 to 20 h.p.

OIL FUELLING BARGE

Employed in the conveyance of fuel oil to ships in harbour, saving them a special visit to the oil depots. She is really a miniature tanker fitted with powerful oil pumps and a tower amidships supporting flexible pipe connections. Dimensions approximately 180 ft. × 40 ft.

OIL SEPARATOR BARGE

A special type of craft, constructed for the purpose of preventing the pollution of dock and canal water by waste oil from ships. This one can deal with 200 tons of water per hour and has an oil-carrying capacity of about 50 tons. Self-propelling, with reciprocating engines.

RHINE BARGE

A very big type of steel barge to be seen on the rivers Rhine, Maas and connecting waterways. When loaded almost awash the Rhineschiff will carry about 1,000 tons. Some are fitted with mast in a tabernacle. The round wheelhouse is a conspicuous feature. Accommodation aft for crew.

CAR FLOAT.

In reality a dumb train ferry—towed from alongside. The one shown operates on the St. Lawrence. She is a box-shaped vessel with two sets of rails and bridge over. To assist manoeuvreability the tug's engines may be controlled from the float by cable. 290 ft. × 45 ft. × 7 ft. 6 ins. draught.

RIVER PLATE CATTLE CARRIER

A vessel constructed for the transport of cattle from up-river estates. The animals are carried on open decks protected by closely-spaced slats. Has motor engines of about 200 h.p. The example shown is a shallow draught ship whose approximate dimensions are 160 ft. × 36 ft. × 6 ft. 8ins.

CLAY SLURRY CARRIER

A ship, in some respects like a small tanker, specially designed to carry liquid clay for cement manufacture. That illustrated is a motorship 170 ft. × 30 ft., carrying 1,000 tons. There are six slurry compartments which are filled by small watertight hatches and discharged through pipes by pumping aparatus.

EUROPEAN CARGO COASTER (Steam)

Of the raised quarterdeck type, this vessel is typical of steamers in the coasting trade. These ships have to face much bad weather, and are also built to lie aground without straining. Machinery being aft allows long, clear holds and big hatches. Dimensions about 190 ft. × 32 ft. × 13 ft.

N. EUROPEAN PASSENGER COASTER

Most of these are very smart little ships with comfortable, though rather cramped, accommodation for about 150 passengers in two classes. Accommodation is usually reduced in winter time, the vacant space being, in some cases, used for cargo. A fair amount of general cargo carried. Approximate measurements : 250 ft. × 35 ft. Tonnage about 1,500.

MOTOR COASTER

Particularly handy little ship, strong enough to cross the North Sea or similar open water, in almost any weather, yet able to nose her way into tiny, out-of-the-way ports, and lie aground without injury. Clear hold, large hatches. Typical dimensions, approximately 125 ft. × 23 ft. Speed about 8½ knots.

PACIFIC PASSENGER COASTER

A distinct contrast to the European type. Has extensive superstructure, with the bridge placed well forward. Employed on services along the Western Canadian and U.S. coasts between the Southern States and Alaska. Tonnage between approximately 1,500 and 4,000. Speed 18 to 20 knots.

THAMES BRIDGE COLLIER

Ships of about 1,300 tons designed to pass under London's bridges. Funnel, mast and ventilators are hinged or telescoped, and she has a large rudder for quick turning. The holds are so built that they can be cleanly emptied by mechanical grabs. Nicknamed 'Flatiron' because of her shape.

SEA-GOING COLLIER

A ship of about 2,000 tons used for the carriage of coal, mainly between British and European ports. Her chief features are big, clear holds and large hatches. Nowadays usually loaded and discharged by shore plant. The example has her machinery amidships, but many have their engines aft.

CONCRETE SHIP

Built in considerable numbers in the United States during the Great War as a means of economising in steel. Had steel keel, stem and stern frame, and a light framework of steel rods. A wooden mould was erected around this and liquid concrete poured in. Sides were about 6 ins. thick.

CORRUGATED SHIP

A ship with longitudinal corrugations in the region of the waterline, running from the turn of the bow to the quarter. Invented in 1906, it is claimed that they give increased cargo capacity, greater stability, and economy owing to reduced propeller slip. Alternatively called 'Monitor Ships.'

CROSS-CHANNEL CARGO VESSEL

Though not much heard of, besides the first class passenger vessels there are a number of smart, fast little cargo ships, carrying chiefly urgent or perishable goods on Channel and short sea routes. On certain services cattle are carried. About 800 to 1,000 tons. Speed 14 to 16 knots.

CROSS-CHANNEL MOTOR SHIP

Of similar size to the steamer, but machinery space and fuel consumption reduced. Saves expense of keeping steam up during wait at terminal ports. Most popular at present where a speed of about 20 knots is sufficient, although much greater speeds have been attained by diesel ships.

CROSS-CHANNEL PADDLE STEAMER

The earliest ships of this type were placed on service about 1820, replacing sailing packets. The later cross-Channel paddlers were fine vessels of considerable speed, and did not become entirely extinct until 1923 when the last two were broken up, unable to compete with the newer screw steamers.

CROSS-CHANNEL PASSENGER SCREW STEAMER

Smart miniature liners of about 2,000 to 3,000 tons, fitted with most comfortable accommodation, many of the night boats having beautiful single or double berth rooms supplied with hot and cold water. Has to be handy, and suitable for much astern working while negotiating harbour entrances, etc. Speed about 25 knots.

RIVER PILOT CUTTER

A small cutter for river work. She puts river pilots aboard incoming ships. Example, stationed in the Thames, is a diesel-engined vessel 48 ft. in length, of particularly strong construction for running alongside moving ships day and night. Special handrails are provided for safety during boarding operations.

SEA-GOING PILOT CUTTER

The steam or diesel-engined sea-going pilot cutter is a fine little ship which cruises off coast or estuary, putting pilots aboard inward-bound vessels, etc. She keeps on her station in all weathers. Transfers pilots by launch. Often resembles a trawler in size and appearance.

U.S. COASTGUARD CUTTER

Employed off American coasts in prevention of smuggling, on Atlantic ice patrol, assisting vessels in distress, etc. Ship illustrated, a cruising cutter about 327 ft. in length, is a twin screw, geared turbine steamer with water tube boilers. Armament in large cutters consists of 5 in., 3 in. and 6-pounder guns.

MOTOR DRIFTER

Has, in many cases, replaced steam type. Chief advantages of this craft are saving of machinery and bunker space, and economy in running as they avoid necessity for keeping steam up when engines are not being used. Example, from Scottish port, has 120 h.p. oil engine.

STEAM DRIFTER

A numerous type of fishing vessel which lowers a vertical net over the bow and drifts to it with her foremast lowered. Has not the ' gallows ' of the trawler, and is fitted with a powerful capstan in place of the trawl winch. Usually has compound engines. Fish capacity about 50 tons.

EXCURSION STEAMER

Lightly-built, fast ships, usually paddle driven. Shallow draught and good manœuvreability for running alongside piers. Example is on Thames Estuary service. She has wide, open decks, but also spacious saloons with large windows for bad weather. The bridge is amidships, just aft of the funnel. Dimensions : 292 ft. × 36 ft. 8 ins.

FABRICATED SHIP

This system of construction was introduced towards the end of the Great War. Having straight sheer line and no complicated hull curves, these vessels could be assembled by unskilled labour, nearly all parts being standardised. Most distinctive feature was the square, triangular stern.

CHAIN FERRY

Ferries across short distances are sometimes built to work themselves along by chains laid between the terminal points. In the example the wheels through which the chains run are driven by Diesel-electric machinery. The vessel is employed on vehicle and passenger service. Length 107 ft. over prows, beam 38 ft. 9 ins.

PASSENGER FERRY

These ships vary a great deal with service and locality. Must be handy and able to take hard knocks when making piers, etc. Heavy rubbing strakes are fitted and wide gangways. Example is from River Mersey, screw steamer, three decks. Has numerous watertight bulkheads. About 152 ft. × 46 ft.

VEHICULAR FERRY

Vary considerably in size and appearance. Example is beamy and square-ended, with clear, open, flush deck. The bridge is high, allowing a clear view fore and aft. Has special wide gangways which, when raised vertically, form gates. Stout rubbing strakes are fitted. Dimensions about 145 ft. × 50 ft. This ship is on the Mersey ferry service.

FINNISH LAKES STEAMER

Strange-looking little ships running on the numerous lakes of Finland. The same type are to be seen on the Gota Canal System. Limited as to size and draught by locks, etc., they are vessels of around 255 to 285 tons. Average dimensions: 97 ft. × 22 ft. Accommodation for about fifty passengers.

FISH CARRIER

A ship used for transporting the catch from a fishing fleet at sea to the market port. The type in this case is similar to the North Sea trawler but rather larger. She is fitted for trawling. Fish is transferred from other trawlers of the fleet by small boats.

FISHERY PATROL VESSEL

Being built for detection and capture of fishing craft breaking regulations, this ship is given the outward appearance of a trawler. Chief differences are that she has a shallow draught aft, is twin screw and much faster than the trawler, and has a motor launch on foredeck hidden by bulwarks.

FLUSH-DECK SHIP

The earliest cargo steamers were completely flush-decked, that is, they had a level, continuous deck from bow to stern with small erections around funnel and engine-room skylight. The 'spar-deck' ship was a development having more elaborate erections amidships. Not so popular as other types, such as the 'Three Island'.

FRUIT CARRIER

The modern motor fruiter is of about 4,000 tons, with high-speed for a freighter (about 16½ knots). Her holds are divided into small, insulated compartments, whose air is kept fresh and at different temperatures to suit various fruits carried. Services mainly between California and European ports.

'GAS' SHIP

The 'Gas ship' is not a type of vessel, but any ship driven by engines burning gas generated on board. This method of propulsion has been developed recently in Germany, where various gas river craft are running successfully. Among fuels used in gas producers are coal, coke, peat, and wood.

GREAT LAKES CANAL FREIGHTER

Similar to the large type of Lakes freighter Has a big rudder for quick manœuvring, and rubbing strakes to protect the hull while negotiating locks, etc. Anchors are housed flush. Cargo handling gear is not usually carried, this work being done by shore plant. Tonnage about 2,000 to 3,000.

LARGE GREAT LAKES FREIGHTER

A bulk cargo carrier. Characteristics: bridge right forward; clear decks; very large hatches; machinery aft; a long 'steering pole' on stem to give the helmsman his direction. Built up to about 20,000 tons deadweight. These ships are usually discharged by extensive shore plant using huge mechanical grabs.

GREAT LAKES PASSENGER STEAMER

A very fine type of special passenger ship. The example is approximately 350 ft. long and has a tonnage of about 4,300. Excellent accommodation for about 400 passengers. Like the Lakes freighter she has the bridge right forward and the funnel aft. Carries a considerable amount of cargo.

GREAT LAKES SELF-DISCHARGING FREIGHTER

Special Lakes type running to ports with no efficient shore plant. Similar to the ordinary Lakes freighter but fitted with various kinds of conveyor belts, cranes, etc. It is possible, by this means, for ship to discharge her own bulk cargo at a rate of nearly 2,000 tons per hour.

HOSPITAL SHIP (Ocean-going)

Employed during wartime in transporting wounded overseas from battle fronts. Fitted out with large wards containing special cots; operating theatres; accommodation for doctors and nursing staff. To distinguish her from other ships such as freighters and transports she is painted white with broad green line and red crosses.

RIVER HOSPITAL SHIP

A miniature hospital mounted on a beamy, shallow-draught hull. The example, built for work in Mesopotamia, has sixty cots, dispensary and operating theatre. A lift is fitted between main and upper decks. She is a twin-screw vessel 150 ft. × 30 ft. × 6 ft. 6 ins. draught. Has ice tanks for tropical conditions.

F

HEALTH AUTHORITY'S LAUNCH

Small vessel used by port medical authorities for examining inward-bound ships and taking off infectious cases. Example, stationed at Gravesend, has accommodation for doctors and miniature hospital on deck for four stretcher cases. Driven by twin Diesel engines giving speed of about 12 knots. Dimensions: 75 ft. × 14 ft. 6 ins.

CARGO LINER

The cargo liner runs to schedule on regular services. Individual ships vary considerably. The example illustrated is an ocean-going vessel on a North Atlantic service. Her dimensions are 512 ft. × 61 ft. 6 ins. Speed 14 knots. 'Goal post' masts allow convenient placing of derricks and speedy handling of cargo.

CRUISING LINER

The thoroughbred pleasure cruiser is built for cruising and nothing else. Has extensive sports decks and much hold space is given over to gymnasia, swimming pools, etc., and passengers have more spacious accommodation than in a ship of similar size on regular service. The example has accommodation for about 1,500 passengers.

PASSENGER LINER (1890)

First class passenger ships of this period were steel, screw vessels, often flush-decked, sometimes with raised forecastle and turtle deck aft. Rigged with two, three or four masts, square-rigged on foremast or fore and main. Compound steam engines. Speed about 18 knots. Dimensions about 500 ft. × 57 ft. 7,500 tons.

FAR EAST PASSENGER LINER

This type, though fitted with first class accommodation, is smaller than her Atlantic counterpart, partly because of Suez Canal restriction. Nor is she so fast. Cabins and ventilation are carefully planned for tropical conditions. Extensive open but shaded decks. Carry cargo. Approximate dimensions: 600 ft. × 73 ft. × 48 ft.   20,000 tons.

CABIN CLASS LINER

Ship of medium size carrying passengers in reasonable comfort at less expense than the big luxury liner. Also has considerable cargo space. About 20,000 tons. Speed in region of 20 knots. Approximate dimensions: 600 ft. × 75 ft. × 27 ft. draught. Recently big vessels have been classed as 'cabin' ships.

MOTOR CARGO LINER

On services where Diesel oil is procurable at economical prices, the motorship has several advantages over the steamer, among them saving of engine and bunker space. These ships are generally fitted with electric deck-winches and other auxiliary machinery. Speed between about 12 and 17 knots.

MOTOR PASSENGER LINER

On a number of services the Diesel-driven ship has almost entirely displaced the steamer. Although many are luxuriously appointed, they are not generally built over about 25,000 tons. The sketch shows a modern, twin-screw ship running on the Southampton-Capetown mail service. Her tonnage is 25,500.

'MAMMOTH' LINER

So-called 'Mammoth' liners are the world's greatest ships, found only on Atlantic services where sufficient wealthy passengers are available. Have luxurious accommodation of first class hotels. Capable of maintaining the fastest regular service in all weathers. Speed about 31 knots. Approximately between 40,000 and 80,000 tons.

ATLANTIC LINER (1840)

Steamships of this period on the Atlantic ferry were paddle-driven, engines being about 750 h.p. Wooden built, they carried mails, about 200 tons of cargo, and just over 100 passengers in accommodation which was considered luxurious at that time. Typical dimensions : 210 ft. × 35 ft.

LOCOMOTIVE CARRIER

Specially designed for the transport of railway engines, rolling stock, light-vessels, barges, etc. The example is a twin-screw motorship of 7,200 tons, capable of taking over fifty railway coaches at one load. Has specially powerful derricks for handling her unusually heavy cargo, and ballasting arrangements which ensure a seaworthy trim.

MAIERFORM SHIP

Ships with maierform bow were first built in Germany. This form is something like a modified yacht bow with curved stem and convex lines. Many ordinary ships have recently been lengthened and altered to maierform, the purpose being to improve speed and behaviour in heavy seas without increased power.

FUNNEL-LESS MOTOR SHIP

The first ocean-going motorships were built without funnels, and there are a number to-day which follow this principle, having their exhaust gas led up the main mast. Usually three or four-masted. The type made its appearance about 1912. Used chiefly for cargo, as unpopular with travelling public.

ORE CARRIER

Bulk ore is an awkward cargo because of its consistency and great weight. If heavy weight is stowed too low in a ship she rolls badly, therefore ore carriers' holds are often in the form of hoppers, unloaded from the bottom. Ore is raised to deck by various mechanical contrivances.

'PUFFER'

A name given to steam lighters employed on the Scottish coasts. These useful little craft are of dimensions which allow them to work through the canals. They sometimes set a triangular sail for use in favourable winds and for steadying. This may be seen stowed against the mast.

RAISED QUARTER DECK VESSEL

A sea-going ship, built with the after deck on a slightly higher level than the fore deck, to give correct trim with full cargo. As this means a break in the longitudinal members, strengthening diaphragm plates are fitted where the change in height occurs. Popular in the European coasting trade.

BEAM ENGINED STEAMER

The beam engine was introduced in America about 1823 and became very popular on Hudson River and coasts. Has a large vertical cylinder connected to paddle shaft by an overhead rocking beam mounted on A-shaped frames. This projects above superstructure and can be seen in the drawing.

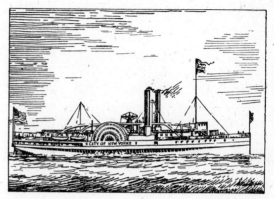

CHINESE RIVER STEAMER

Carries passengers and cargo chiefly on the Yangtse river. She is a beamy, shallow-draught vessel, having open decks fitted with awnings or other shelter. Stern-wheel or propellers in tunnels. The example is a twin screw ship. Approximate dimensions are : length 198 ft., beam 33 ft. Built 1924.

HUDSON RIVER PASSENGER STEAMER

Large, fast screw or paddle steamer of shallow draught running with passengers between various points on the Hudson. She is a distinctly American type, with superimposed open decks, having a slight family likeness to the Mississipi passenger vessel. Dimensions of example : 260 ft. 6 ins. × 60 ft. 1,721 tons.

MISSISSIPPI PASSENGER STEAMER

Example, side paddle vessel, specially designed with little freeboard and shallow draught. She has elaborate superstructure and fancy smoke-stack tops, the stacks being placed side by side. These ships often had three decks. Gangways are suspended over the bows. Used to have keen races and attained considerable speed.

NILE RIVER STEAMER

Shallow draught vessels, either paddle or sternwheel, in the region of 150 to 250 ft. in length. They have spacious promenade decks and excellent cabin accommodation, many of the rooms being fitted with hot and cold water. A large number of these boats are run by the tourist agencies.

STERN-WHEEL RIVER STEAMER

Beamy, shallow-draught vessels employed principally on the rivers Mississippi, Niger, Nile, St. Lawrence and Yangtse. Instead of propulsion being from the sides as in the ordinary paddle steamer, there is one wide paddle wheel across the stern, driven by rods from a pair of horizontal cylinders.

THAMES UP-RIVER STEAMER

A comfortable pleasure craft carrying passengers during the summer season. Has large awninged deck space and saloon. Seven knots is about maximum speed for these craft owing to wash in narrow reaches. The example is 105 ft. × 16 ft. 6 ins. Built of steel frames and teak planking. Passenger capacity about 350.

ROTOR SHIP

Invented by Herr Anton Flettner in 1924. The circular towers were rotated by motor engines and obtained propulsive power from the wind. Had auxiliary engine and propeller for use in calms. Two ships have been tried, but they were a commercial failure and have been adapted for ordinary propulsion.

SALVAGE VESSEL

Salvage work requires a stout, handy ship, able to stand any weather. She must have strong, reliable engines. Fitted with powerful winches, hawsers and all towing gear, fire and salvage pumps. Also on certain jobs complete equipment for deep-sea divers is installed. Trawlers are sometimes converted for this service.

SLUDGE VESSEL

A special type of ship built for the transport and disposal of sewage from large ports. The one illustrated, belonging to the London County Council, is a very smart little craft about 250 ft. in length. She has small, airtight hatches and special valve arrangements for discharge.

SCOTTISH MOTOR SMACK

Class of fishing vessel largely replacing the smaller steam and sailing craft. Propelled by petrol, paraffin or Diesel engines. Excellent sea boat. Hull is divided into three sections : crews' quarters, fish hold and engine-room. There is a small wheelhouse aft. Mast in tabernacle. Average length : 45 to 50 ft.

EARLY STEAMBOAT

Man's earliest efforts in steam propulsion afloat took many forms, but all used some form of paddle. Illustrated is the first steamboat to be used in Europe, built in 1812. Had thin, tall funnel on which a square sail was sometimes set. Her dimensions were 40 ft. 3 ins. × 11 ft. 3 ins.

TIMBER CARRIER

Although many ordinary tramp steamers carry wood cargoes, a special type has been developed for this purpose. To take large deck loads she has long clear well decks with derricks at extreme bow and stern, and at each end of midship superstructure. Between about 1,000 and 2,000 tons.

MISSISSIPPI TOWBOAT

A beamy, shallow-draught ship fitted with special towing knees forward so that she can push her tow of about six barges, containing in all perhaps 10,000 tons of freight. The one shown has twin screws, but many are stern wheelers. Crew of fifteen to thirty men according to size of boat.

TRAIN FERRY (Closed Type)

Employed as a link in railway systems where wide lakes or channels must be crossed, often in bad weather. Seaworthy, ship-shape bow, sometimes icebreaker. High sides and deck over trains for protection. Two or more sets of rails. Trains run on from stern. About 350 ft. × 58 ft.

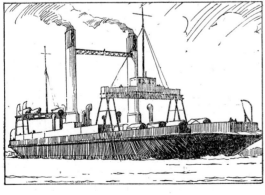

TRAIN FERRY (Open Type)

Employed on services having good weather conditions; therefore an enclosed ship is unnecessary. The rail deck layout is similar to that of the closed type, but in many cases double-ended so that trains run on one end, off at the other. In both types funnels are usually at sides.

TRAMP STEAMER

Goes all over the world picking up chance cargoes. Must be of handy size, economical, able to load with her own derricks, as out-of-the-way ports may have no shore plant. The modern tramp is much more scientifically designed than those of Kipling's day. Speed 9 to 11 knots.

MISSION TRAWLER

Special service vessel employed by a society which ministers to deep-sea fishing fleets. Carries missionaries, also various comforts for the fishermen. Fitted for trawling to help pay her way. Example is similar to ordinary steam trawler, but forward of the fish hold is a missionaries' cabin and bathroom.

MOTOR TRAWLER

Internal combustion engines have advantages over steam for trawlers, and have been installed in a large number of boats. As a slow-running propeller is required for trawling, it is usual to fit reduction gearing. An electric winch is fitted for the trawl. The sketch shows a large French trawler.

STEAM TRAWLER (Icelandic Type)

Work around Iceland and the Newfoundland banks. Larger than the North Sea type, as they have further to go, and may meet more severe conditions. Their general lines are similar to the smaller boats, but the superstructure is more elaborate, and they are fitted with long-range radio and refrigerators.

STEAM TRAWLER (North Sea Type)

Strong, good sea boats approximately 100 ft. × 23 ft. with powerful engines enabling her to drag a heavy trawl and remain at sea in all weathers. Fitted with a large trawl winch and portable divisions on deck for sorting fish. The hold is sub-divided and has shelves for stowage of fish on ice.

TROOPSHIP

A vessel employed on the carriage of troops overseas for service on foreign stations. The modern example is specially designed with spacious accommodation for about 1,500 officers and men. Separate berths provided for families, also a large hospital. Passengers are carried out of the trooping season. Tonnage about 12,000.

TRUNK DECK SHIP

A cargo vessel very similar to the turret-deck ship, but with square instead of rounded gunwales. Central 'trunk' is more of an erection than integral part of hull. Few built. Suitable chiefly for the carriage of bulk grain, as to some extent self-trimming.

AMERICAN TUG

In general appearance the American vessel differs considerably from the corresponding British type, having extensive superstructure and towing bitts well aft instead of the midship hook of the English tug. Usually has a specially strengthened bow to enable her to push the tow ahead. Also does much towing alongside.

CANAL AND RIVER TUG

A small tug, employed chiefly in the towing of barges in docks, canals, etc. This type has a hinged funnel and mast to enable her to pass under low bridges. Has very little crew accommodation as she seldom works at night. May be either steam or motor.

OCEAN GOING TUG (Steam)

A large, powerful vessel with high forecastle so that she can remain at sea in any weather. Fitted with reciprocating engines, also fire and salvage pumps. Employed on long-towage and salvage. The Dutch specialise in this class of work. Average size between 100 ft. and 200 ft. long.

PADDLE TUG

A type now rarely seen. Its particular work is the manœuvring of large vessels in confined spaces. Lashed alongside, rapid turning is achieved. No paddle tugs have been built for some years, but quite a number are still at work in various parts of the world.

RHINE TUG

Tugs in use on the River Rhine, towing huge barges, are of most distinctive appearance. Long, low craft with widely-spaced funnels and usually a large anchor prominently suspended from the bow. Generally paddle, but some of the latest tugs are Diesel-driven screw vessels.

SEA-GOING TUG

Her work consists of the docking of ships and general estuary or coastal towage. Similar to the ocean type, but smaller and without raised forecastle. A crew of six or eight is carried. The galley is usually under the bridge, with accommodation forward and aft. Approximately 60 to 100 ft. in length.

TURRET-DECK SHIP

A vessel without sheer. The top of the hull proper is at the rounded 'turret' deck. Above this there is a narrow structure running fore and aft. Now obsolete. Were used for carriage of grain and paid reduced Suez Canal dues. Had great longitudinal strength with few hold pillars.

VOITH-SCHNEIDER VESSEL

Ships of various types have recently been built with Voith-Schneider propellers, by which the vessel is both propelled and steered. Propeller revolves in vertical axis, and has six vertical blades in circle. Alteration in angle of blades changes direction of thrust. Ship can turn in own length.

WAR DEPARTMENT VESSEL

Ship of coaster type belonging to the British War Department with chief depot at Woolwich. She is employed in the transport of guns, explosives, stores, etc. around the coast and to other Government vessels requiring supplies. The accompanying sketch shows a motor example. Dimensions: 95 ft. × 19ft. 8 knots.

WATER 'BUS

The service of these boats on river and harbour is analogous to that of the motor road 'bus ashore. This example has seating accommodation for 115 passengers, in threes facing the bow. Twin Diesel engines give a speed of 14 knots. Length, 72 ft ; beam, 14 ft. ; draught, 4 ft. 3 ins.

WHALE CATCHER

Of forty to ninety tons, built on similar lines to the steam trawler. Forward is a harpoon-gun, and the foremast carries a crow's nest. The hull is divided into crew spaces, hold for harpoon-lines, bunkers, stokehold and engine-room. Crew about twelve. Sometimes called a ' Gun Boat.'

WHALE FACTORY-SHIP

Ship 15,000 to 20,000 tons, to which ' catchers ' bring carcases for treatment. Has slipway in stern and powerful gear for hauling whales on deck. Blubber is stripped and carcase cut up with steam saws. Between decks machinery for extracting oils, etc. is installed. Acts as parent ship for fleet of ' catchers.'

MOTOR YACHT

Similar to the steam yacht, whose place it has largely taken, but driven by Diesel engines. Size up to about 2,000 tons. Often most luxuriously fitted. The one illustrated is 165 ft. × 26 ft. and 11 ft. draught. Tonnage about 450. Advantages—cleanliness and saving of cost of keeping steam up in port.

ROYAL YACHT

Yachts were owned by royalty in the 17th century, and since then have varied in size and type. The British example, the world's largest yacht, was built in 1899, and is used on ceremonial occasions such as naval reviews. Tonnage 4,700 and speed when new was around 20 knots.

STEAM YACHT

Large type of power-driven yacht used for pleasure cruising. May be of any size up to about 3,000 tons. Elaborately fitted out with often extremely luxurious accommodation for owner and a large number of guests. Usually carries motor launches, dinghies, etc. Almost invariably painted white with yellowish funnel.

BUOYAGE VESSEL

A special-service ship used for putting down and taking up buoys, mooring lightships, etc. A handy vessel with tripod mast, strong derricks and sheaves at bow enabling her to lift heavy weights. Twin Diesel engines give 12 knots speed. Buoys are carried on well deck. Dimensions: 173 ft. × 33 ft.

CABLESHIP

Job is the laying and repair of submarine cables. Has a hold for stowage of mark buoys, etc., and several circular tanks holding cable coiled round central cones. Sheaves are fitted at bow and stern for taking in or paying out cable, also powerful windlasses for working it. Special grapnels are used to pick up cable from the sea bed.

G

C-2 CARGO VESSEL

One of the three classes of modern ships built to the requirements of the U.S. Maritime Commission. Among their chief features are high speed—15½ knots—and extremely low fuel consumption. The example is a steam turbine ship, but some of the class are diesel driven. Approximate dimensions : 460 ft. × 63 ft., 6,000 tons.

CROSS-CHANNEL STEAMER (Tropical)

The vessel illustrated operates under semi-tropical conditions, running between Monte-video and Buenos Aires. Passengers are accommodated as far as possible in outside cabins on the superstructure decks, and particular attention has been paid to the problem of efficient ventilation. To suit local conditions her draught is only 10 ft.

MOTOR TANK BARGE

The example is a very efficient little vessel, specially designed to carry petrol in bulk. There are five cargo tanks, and the crew's quarters forward are fitted with fireproof electric heaters and cooking apparatus. Approximate dimensions: 115 ft. × 21 ft. 6 ins. × 8 ft. 9 ins. Speed about 8 knots. Carrying capacity 285 tons. Can tow a dumb barge.

WHALEBACK STEAMER

A 'freak' Great Lakes grain carrier, now obsolete. It was thought that the 'whaleback' had great advantages over the ordinary ship, but this was disproved under service conditions. The exposed deckhouses were liable to damage, and the bow shape was very unsatisfactory in a heavy sea.

SMALL POWER

SMALL POWER

THE tremendous increase in numbers of small power-driven vessels has been due to the great advances made with the internal combustion engine. Before the motor power unit appeared, the only mechanically propelled small craft were steam picket boats, launches, and a few electrically driven boats.

Perfection of a planing hull form in conjunction with light, fast running motor engines has resulted in the construction of numerous small naval speed craft. Motor pinnaces, barges, launches, torpedo boats, tenders, to mention only a few, are all in regular service, the majority being carried by the larger fighting ships.

In the Royal National Lifeboat Institution and many similar foreign services, motor boats of various types have almost entirely replaced the old pulling and sailing craft, their engines being able, if necessary, to run when completely submerged. In some of these boats the engine stops automatically if capsized.

Outboard units are popular for light racing and pleasure craft as they are very economical as regards fuel and may be changed from one boat to another and stored out of the weather when not in use.

S M A L L   P O W E R

MOTOR CABIN CRUISER

A popular and varied type of small yacht for sea and estuary cruising at about 8 knots. Example is 30 ft. × 9 ft. with draught 3 ft. Wooden built, twin screw. There is just over 6 ft. headroom in accommodation, which consists of stateroom with two berths, saloon, galley and lavatory.

HYDROGLYDER

Light, fast speed craft propelled by an air-screw instead of an under-water Propeller. Have been developed chiefly in Italy and the United States, and speeds over 80 miles an hour have been attained. The example, from Italy, has dimensions 20 ft. × 7 ft. 4 ins. with an engine of 120 h.p.

HYDROPLANE

A light, shallow racing craft built of wood or metal alloy. The propeller is placed some distance below the hull, and a small fin is fitted under the bottom forward to assist steering. Cushioned seat and car type steering wheel are used. Attains high speeds in the popular trophy races.

CUSTOMS LAUNCH

Service launch enabling customs officers to visit ships lying in a river or harbour. Powerful motor boat with forward steering position, small cabin and cockpit. A rubbing band and rope fenders are fitted to protect the hull when boarding. The boat illustrated, about 40 ft. long, is used on the Thames.

DESTROYER'S LAUNCH

Fast, hard-chine launch carried by destroyers and used as tender, etc. That illustrated is 25 ft. in length with a speed of about 25 knots. Has three watertight bulkheads and automatic bailers are fitted. Cabin forward, open cockpit aft protected by a spray hood. To carry about nine persons.

THAMES POLICE LAUNCH

Used for the detection of theft and other crimes among Thames shipping, silent approach is important. The engine casing is lined with sound-insulating [material, also a special silencer is fitted. In touch with headquarters by wireless. The example, 28 ft. × 7 ft. 6 ins., has a Diesel engine. Speed about 14 knots.

RIVER LAUNCH

A shallow-draught, runabout craft with large cockpit which, in some boats, contains one or two loose chairs. The example has a car-type hood, side screens and steering wheel. Her engine is housed under the fore deck. The flat stern leaves very little wash. Length, 20 to 30 ft.

SERVICE LAUNCH

A powerful motor launch well protected by fenders and fitted with towing bitts. These boats vary considerably, and are employed on all kinds of general service in connection with shipping. The example has a search-light and large cabin. Has to bear many hard knocks. Length about 40 ft.

STEAM LAUNCH

An early type of mechanically-propelled boat used on rivers and occasionally as a yacht's tender. She had a small boiler with tall funnel, exhaust pipe and pressure gauge. In the majority of these craft the machinery was more or less exposed. Length about 15 to 30 ft.

MOTOR LIFEBOAT

This type of boat, which has become almost universal, has powerful engines, and in many cases a watertight cabin in which rescued may be kept warm and dry. Built to various designs and sizes to suit local conditions. Twin screw, the propellers working in tunnels. Keep running even if submerged.

SHIP'S MOTOR LIFEBOAT

These boats are propelled by engines of about 30 h.p., giving a speed of 7 to 8 knots. Fitted with wireless, searchlights and electric heaters. Used for towing or assisting ordinary pulling boats. One or more motor boats are now carried by all large passenger liners, and one or two of the largest vessels have all motor lifeboats.

STEAM LIFEBOAT

A larger boat than the sailing type. The screws work in tunnels to avoid damage, and the engines are kept as watertight as possible. Stations with suitable conditions for steam boats are very few and only about half a dozen have ever been built in Britain.

OUTBOARD MOTOR BOAT

No engine is installed in this boat, but she is driven by a light, portable combined propelling and steering unit which is clamped to the transom. A most handy method of propulsion for dinghies and small racing hydroplanes. Horse power between about $1\frac{1}{2}$ and 25. Weight 29 lbs. upwards.

BRITISH COLUMBIAN SALMON BOAT

The Columbian salmon canning industry employs these ugly but efficient little vessels. A seine net is used, shot from a pivoted platform at the stern. A boom is fitted for handling the catch. The boat illustrated has a Diesel engine which gives her a speed of about 8 knots.

MOTOR SAMPAN

In modern Chinese ports the motor sampan is, to some extent, replacing the ancient type. The example has dimensions 40 ft. $\times$ 9 ft. 3 ins. $\times$ 2 ft. draught, and is used on the Yangtse Kiang. Two Diesel engines are fitted, the propellers working in a tunnel. Speed about 9 knots.

ADMIRAL'S BARGE

A speed craft of the Navy. Contains a fore cockpit and admiral's cabin, wheel-house and another cockpit in the stern. Speed approximately 22 knots. A spare engine is carried which can be quickly changed if one of those in use should break down. Length about 45 ft.

ROYAL AIR FORCE TARGET BOAT

Armoured speedboat, 37 ft. 6 ins. long, with three 100 h.p. engines mounted abreast. She is used for dummy bomb practice. The foredeck is unprotected, but the interior is filled with a buoyant substance so that a bomb can pass right through the boat without causing sufficient damage to sink her.

AIRCRAFT REFUELLING TENDER

The duty of this craft is to refuel flying boats or seaplanes floating on the water in harbour. The example belongs to the Royal Air Force. A 25 ft. boat. Freeboard is kept low so that there is no difficulty in passing under the wings of the aircraft.

ROYAL AIR FORCE TENDER

Powerful, twin-engined craft employed for general purposes on Royal Air Force coast stations at home and abroad. She is capable of a speed of about 23 knots, the engines being of 100 h.p. each. The boats have a cruising radius of about 200 miles, should this be necessary.

R.A.F. RESCUE LAUNCH

A powerful speed launch about 64 ft. in length, used to rescue airmen brought down in the sea. Painted black with yellow decks. Accommodation provides for badly injured men, and crew of eight. Wireless and radio-direction finder installed. Good sea boats. Speed about 40 knots. The Navy employs similar vessels.

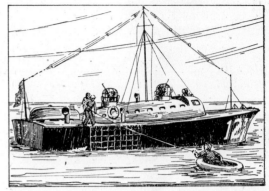

COASTAL MOTOR BOAT

High speed, shallow-draught type torpedo boat which did a variety of useful work during the Great War. They were built in three sizes : 40 ft., 55 ft. and 70 ft., and were armed with torpedoes, Lewis guns or depth charges according to the size of boat and service required. Speed 30 to 41 knots.

SEA SLED

This type of craft was experimented with a good many years ago but not developed. It has been revived recently, and the one illustrated, used by the U.S. Navy for high-speed rescue work, etc., has attained over 45 knots. Hull is in form of a double V. 45 ft. long.

TORPEDO RETRIEVING LAUNCH

Employed by the British Admiralty for finding and towing in spent torpedoes, the example is a motor craft 35 ft. × 9 ft. Has stout teak hull with metal sheathing. Winch fitted in cockpit and sheaves on transom for raising torpedoes to surface, and special bollards on deck for towing it alongside.

WARSHIPS

WARSHIPS

MANY of the early iron and steel men-of-war were failures. Faulty design made them top-heavy, terrible sea boats, slow and unwieldy. Indeed it is a fact that not a few of the so-called sea-going ships spent practically the whole of their active existences in harbour. But during recent years the design of fighting ships has improved enormously and their performance has been influenced by several innovations.

The adoption of oil firing in place of coal, together with improved propelling machinery, has given ships a wider radius of action on a given amount of fuel. It has also had the effect of altering quite considerably the strategic position of certain nations which are dependent upon oil imported by sea, as they must protect the shipping routes and sources of supply.

Developments in aircraft have necessitated increased protection against air attack and the mounting of more efficient anti-aircraft armament. Practically all large war vessels now carry two or more planes of their own. In addition, an entirely new type has been born—the Aircraft Carrier.

The passing of every year shows an increase in the use of welding as opposed to rivetting in hull construction. Is is probable that many future vessels will be almost entirely welded.

WARSHIPS

AIRCRAFT CARRIER

A naval vessel serving as a sea-going aero-drome. Characteristics are a clear deck for taking off and landing, and placing of super-structure on the extreme starboard side. Large hangars are incorporated in the hull, housing about fifty to eighty planes, these being raised to the deck by electric lifts.

ANTI-AIRCRAFT SHIP

The example, first ship in the world to specialize in anti-aircraft work, is one of two old British 'C' class cruisers converted in 1935. Her ordinary armament was replaced by eight 4 in. A.A. guns, one multiple pom-pom, and several smaller guns. Speed 29 knots. Displacement 4,290 tons. Feature is big square control top.

BATTLE CRUISER

A large fighting ship having greater speed than the battleship, but rather lighter armour protection and gun power. A British type, the example is a vessel of 32,000 tons dis-placement. Armament: Six 15 in. guns; twenty-one 4 in.; eight 4 in. anti-aircraft; torpedo tubes. Her speed is just over 30 knots.

BRITISH BATTLESHIP

The latest ships of this type are of 35,000 tons displacement, their main armament consisting of ten 14 in. guns in three turrets as follows : 4-2-4. Official speed is given as 30 knots. Like all large modern fighting ships they carry aircraft and have powerful anti-aircraft armament.

BATTLESHIP OF 1900

The example is a British ship of 15,000 tons displacement, launched 1898. Has the two closely-spaced funnels and equal masts with round fighting tops usual at this period. Heaviest gun, 12 in., 50 tons in weight, and considerable secondary armament. Painted in black, white and buff.

UNITED STATES BATTLESHIP

In these ships the extensive overhang of bow is a distinctive feature. The early lattice steel masts have been replaced by a single mast and 'piled up' control positions. Tonnage between 30,000 and 35,000. 14 in. or 16 in. guns, usually in triple turrets. Speed around 21 knots. Three aircraft are carried.

U.S. BATTLESHIP (1911)

American battleships of this period were distinctive in appearance by reason of their tall lattice steel masts. These have since been found insufficiently steady under modern conditions and are replaced by the tripod type in later ships. Approximate dimensions : 560 ft. × 106 ft. × 26 ft. draught. Tonnage about 26,000. Speed 21 knots.

COAST DEFENCE VESSEL

A beamy, shallow-draught war vessel rather similar to the monitor. The tall control tower amidships and high-angle guns are distinctive features. The ship illustrated belongs to Finland. She is of 3,900 tons displacement. Guns : four 10 in. ; eight 4.7 in. Her speed is about 15½ knots.

NAVAL COLLIER

Built for coaling warships. The use of oil fuel having become general, their place has been taken by the fleet tanker or 'Oiler'. The most prominent feature is the large number of derricks for rapid transference of cargo. The example is of 19,000 tons, belonging to the U.S. Navy.

CORVETTE (Modern)

Recent revival of an old name, applied to one of our latest small warship types. Somewhat like a whale catcher in some particulars, with one or more guns of about 4-in. calibre, and light anti-aircraft armament, she is used for anti-submarine and escort work. Of about 500 tons displacement.

STEAM CORVETTE

Vessels of this type were among the earliest warships to be fitted with screw propellers. Corvettes were lightly armed cruisers. The ship illustrated, of the transitional period between sail and steam, was a screw steamer with ram bow. Painted in black and white with buff funnel.

AIRCRAFT-CARRYING CRUISER

A compromise between the cruiser and aircraft carrier, but much smaller than the latter, this ship of the Swedish Navy is a vessel of 4,755 tons displacement. Armament: six 6 in. guns; four 3 in. anti-aircraft guns; six 21 in. torpedo tubes. She carries six aircraft. Speed 27 knots.

BRITISH CRUISER

The example, a 9,000 ton ship of the Southampton class, has twelve 6 in. guns in triple turrets, eight 4 in. anti-aircraft guns, eight torpedo tubes, etc. She carries three planes in hangars in the superstructure. Speed about 32 knots. Built 1936. There are seven vessels of this class.

CRUISER OF 1900

The example is a British first class cruiser of 11,000 tons displacement. Twin screw ship, speed about 20 knots. Armament comprised sixteen guns of 6 in. calibre or over, twenty smaller guns and two torpedo tubes. Full complement 600 men. Torpedo nets are fitted. Dimensions: 435 ft. × 69 ft. × 26 ft. draught.

ITALIAN CRUISER

Modern example is a distinctive ship with compact, low superstructure and cowled funnels. Her control tower is reduced to a minimum. She is a vessel of 7,283 tons displacement. Speed, 36 knots. Eight 6 in. guns, six 3.9 in. anti-aircraft, six torpedo tubes. Three aircraft are carried.

JAPANESE CRUISER

Although Japanese have adopted Western methods and design in shipbuilding, several features of the cruiser illustrated are unorthodox, notably the complex sheer line. Her particulars are as follows: 9,850 tons; ten 8 in. guns, four 4.7 in. anti-aircraft, eight torpedo tubes. Carries four planes. Speed 32 knots.

NAVAL DEPOT SHIP

Employed as a parent ship for destroyers or submarines, this vessel is capable of supplying a whole flotilla with practically all its supplies, provisions and fuel. Also, she can do most running repairs, and gives crews of small craft relief from their cramped quarters. Example about 15,000 tons.

EARLY DESTROYER

The torpedo boat destroyer was first introduced about 1893. She was larger and faster than the torpedo boat. Armed with comparatively heavy guns, also torpedo tubes. First were ships of about 250 tons displacement. In later boats speed was much increased by fitting turbine engines.

DESTROYER (Tribal Class)

These ships, bearing such names as ' Afridi ', ' Cossack ', etc., are among the larger British destroyers. The semi-clipper stem is a departure from previous practice, also the twin mounting of guns. Extra gun power has been obtained at the expense of torpedo armament. Eight 4.7 in. guns, four 21 in. torpedo tubes. Displacement ; 1,850 tons. Speed, 36 knots.

H

FRENCH DESTROYER

Rather bigger than the average British destroyer, armed with fewer but rather heavier guns. The funnel tops are a distinctive feature in appearance. The example is a vessel of approximately 2,570 tons displacement with a speed of 37 knots. Armament: five 5.5 in. guns and nine 21 in. torpedo tubes.

DREADNOUGHT

The illustration shows H.M.S. Dreadnought, a battleship built in 1906. She was a tremendous advance on other fighting ships of her day, and subsequent ships of the same type were called dreadnoughts. She was fitted with steam turbines giving a speed of 21 knots. Mounted ten 12 in. guns.

RIVER GUNBOAT

A shallow-draught war vessel used for up-river work. The example, stationed in China, is a unit of the British Navy. Her displacement is 185 tons and she carries a crew of 35. Armament: one 3.7 in. howitzer and nine smaller guns. Twin screw. Reciprocating engines. Speed 11¼ knots.

SEA-GOING GUNBOAT

An unprotected, lightly-armed war vessel of about 800 tons displacement, though they varied a good deal. The one illustrated was a British ship, built in 1899. Heaviest gun 4 in., with one or two of smaller calibre. Served for several years on the American and West Indian stations.

IRONCLAD

A warship whose vital parts were protected by heavy iron sheathing, though the hull might be of wood. First introduced by the French about the year 1850. It was not long before a number were built for other navies. They were superseded by steel ships.

'M.L.' (1941)

A new type of small war vessel employed on convoy protection and other duties. She is a flush decked ship, about 120 ft. in length. It is not possible to give many details about this type at the present time, but she is fitted with the latest anti-submarine weapons including depth charges.

NAVAL TRAWLER

Ship of large trawler type with a speed of about $11\frac{1}{2}$ knots. Originally fitted with main mast, but this has been removed to give clear view for light A.A. armament aft of the funnel. Used for anti-submarine and mine-sweeping work. One 4-in. gun forward, Lewis or similar guns in bridge wings. 500 to 600 tons.

SLOOP MINESWEEPER

These vessels are usually of about 700 to 800 tons displacement. The one illustrated is a unit of the British fleet. She has a speed of about 17 knots and is armed with two 4 in. guns. During the Great War large numbers of trawlers were used for this work. The modern Corvette has taken on many of the duties of these ships.

MOTOR MINESWEEPER

These boats are a comparatively recent development in naval architecture. The example is a unit of the British navy and her particulars are as follows: dimensions, 75 ft. × 14 ft. × 5 ft. draught. Driven by three 500 h.p., 12-cylinder petrol engines, giving a speed of 17 knots running free and about 10 when sweeping.

MONITOR

A beamy, shallow-draught war vessel, armed with long-range guns on a high mounting. Employed chiefly on coast bombardment, in which the elevated position of the guns enables them to fire across low land, etc. The example is 405 ft. × 88 ft. and of 8,000 tons displacement.

NETLAYER

Built to lay defensive net barrage as protection for a fleet at anchor. Example is a beamy ship with special bows and sheaves for retrieving nets. Also used for target towing. Dimensions, 310 ft. × 53 ft., 2,860 tons displacement. Has geared turbines, 18 knots. Two 4 in. anti-aircraft guns.

MOTOR PICKET BOAT

A small naval vessel of many uses. The one illustrated is 45 ft. in length, and has four motor engines, giving her a speed of about 23 knots. A machine gun can be mounted on the fore deck, and depth charge throwing or minesweeping gear may be fitted. at a pinch, this boat is capable of carrying 100 men.

STEAM PICKET BOAT

A warship's boat superseded by motor boats. Employed as a tender, etc. The funnel may be lowered, and a light gun-mounting is fitted on the foredeck. Hull divided as follows : chain locker ; fore cabin ; boiler-room ; engine-room ; after cabin and cockpit. Two sizes : 50 ft. and 45 ft.

'Q' SHIP

'Q' or 'Mystery' ships were small merchant vessels, fitted with concealed guns which could be brought to bear by dropping deckhouse sides, etc. Employed as submarine decoys during the Great War. Even sailing coasters were taken over by the Admiralty for this purpose, and met with considerable success.

SUBMARINE

Small war vessel whose chief object is to travel under water and attack enemy surface craft with torpedoes. One or more guns on deck. Fitted with jumping wires to prevent fouling obstructions. Propelled by Diesel engines on surface, electric motors when submerged. Dive and surface by means of horizontal rudders and water ballast.

TARGET SHIP

An obsolete vessel employed as a target for naval gun practice. The one illustrated is a battleship, disarmed and entirely controlled by wireless from an accompanying destroyer. Damage inflicted is generally superficial and can quickly be repaired. Speed and steering are controlled without a man being on board.

NAVAL TARGET

Targets for naval gunnery practice vary considerably in size and construction, according to the size of guns to be exercised. The example, of large size, is an upright wooden lattice erection on a flat raft. It is towed some distance astern of a naval tug or other vessel.

SPAR TORPEDO BOAT

Various small steam craft were fitted with spar torpedoes towards the end of last century. The 'torpedo', extended on a 42 ft. spar, contained about 32 lbs. of guncotton, and was thrust against the enemy ship about 12 ft. below surface. Fired electrically. Became obsolete with the invention of the Whitehead torpedo.

MOTOR TORPEDO BOAT

This little high-speed craft is a revival of the C.M.B. and similar types used during the Great War. On service in British, Italian and other navies. Hard-chine boat armed with two torpedoes and light guns. About 43 knots with full load. Approximately 50 to 70 ft. long.

SECOND CLASS TORPEDO BOAT

This boat, in commission in 1880, was 60 ft. × 8 ft. Armed with a light gun and two torpedoes the latter being carried at each side in cradles. The torpedo was set and started in the cradle, and then released by special dropping gear. Boats of rather later date, slightly larger, with bow tube instead of dropping gear, were to be found in the world's smaller navies until quite recently.

TORPEDO FIRING BOAT

This high-speed craft is used by the British naval authorities for the experimental firing and running of torpedoes, in which work she is more handy and economical than a destroyer. She is a 68 ft. boat with a destroyer type tube mounted on deck just abaft the enclosed steering position.

TURRET SHIP

A type of war vessel introduced during the latter half 19th century, having guns mounted in revolving turrets. The example was of 7,790 tons, launched for British navy in 1869. Low freeboard, guns in twin turrets on centre line. Armoured iron hull. Speed 14 knots. Teak deck protected with plating.

'DIDO' CLASS CRUISER

A class of ten British cruisers completed in 1941. Features are the three-stepped turrets forward, and the main armament of ten 5.25 guns, a calibre not previously used in cruisers. One aircraft is carried, and launched from a catapult. Tonnage is 5,450. Speed 33 knots.

DESTROYER ('Lightning' Class)

The largest British destroyer class. Sixteen ships in the class. Armed with six 4.7-in. guns in gas-tight houses and torpedo tubes in quintuple armoured mountings, also several smaller guns. These ships and the 'Javelin' class are the only single funnelled British destroyers at the present time. Tonnage about 1,920 to 1,935.

DESTROYER (U.S.A.)

The example is one of a large number built between 1917 and 1920. Fifty of these ships were handed over to Great Britain in 1940 for service with the Royal Navy. They are of flush deck type, of approximately 1,100 tons. Armament, four 4-in. guns ; one 3-in. A.A. gun ; twelve torpedo tubes. Designed speed 35 knots.

'KIL' CLASS GUNBOAT

Ships built during the Great War for general patrol work. Double ended to confuse an approaching enemy as to their movements. Several were converted into merchant ships after the war. Armed with one 4.7 in. gun. Single screw vessels with a speed of 13 knots. Approximate dimensions ; 180 ft. × 30 ft. × 11 ft. 9 ins. draught.

'P' CLASS PATROL BOAT

A number of these ships were built during the Great War for escort, patrol and anti-submarine work. In addition to armament of one 4 in. gun and one 2 in. pom-pom, they had a ram bow and carried depth charges. Had low freeboard, but were good sea boats. Turbine, twin screw. Speed about 21 knots. 613 tons displacement.

SUBMARINE (Minelaying)

Only able to lay a limited number of mines of small size, but can work more secretly than a surface ship. Cannot carry a full load of mines and torpedoes at the same time. Example is one of British ' Porpoise ' class. Armament ; One 4 in. gun, six torpedo tubes. Surface speed 15½ knots.

MISCELLANEOUS

MISCELLANEOUS

THIS section contains a queer assortment of craft, many of which, since they have no motive power and have to be towed from place to place, cannot be included among either sailing or power vessels.

But in spite of this and although for the most part they are unsightly objects, they render indispensable service to ordinary shipping. How could heavy masts, boilers, etc., be raised from or into position without the aid of the sheer-hulk or, later, the floating crane? What would be the state of dock-water with all the oily discharge of power-driven vessels but for the Oil Separator Barge? These are but two examples chosen at random from many special service craft to whose humble but untiring efforts the world's shipping owes so much.

The 'Hulk' family in all its forms—coaling, powder, etc.—must surely be the most unhappy of vessels. If, as so many seamen believe, ships have souls, how they must dread the prospect of ever being relegated to the humiliating status of 'hulk.' The only exceptions, possibly, are those used for training purposes; in this capacity they may well take a pride in the part they play in turning out new generations of young sailormen.

MISCELLANEOUS

DUMB BARGE

The barges illustrated are of standard Thames type. 85 ft. long and about 22 ft. in breadth, built of steel. Flat-bottomed, almost double-ended except for a central fin at the stern. Large numbers of these and similar craft are used where cargoes must be carried from ships up river or canal.

CHINESE CATTLE BOAT

Large, shallow draught river boats employed in the transport of cattle downstream. In the bow are six oars, while on the after deck stands the helmsman, skilfully working the huge tiller. The cattle are carried on the main deck amidships. The length of the craft is about 50 to 60 ft.

COMPARTMENT BOAT

Vessel, or train of vessels, used on canals for carrying coal. Rectangular in shape, each section, 20 ft. × 15 ft. × 8 ft., can carry about 35 tons on a 6 ft. draught. A train of a dozen or more, with bow section at head, may be towed by a single tug.

MODERN REVENUE CUTTER

This fast, modern craft is very different from her sailing ancestor. Probably called by different names such as 'Patrol Cruiser', etc. Example employed by Canadian authorities on St. Lawrence and nearby coasts. Hull of aluminium alloy, two Diesel engines. Speed about 20 knots. Length 65 ft.

BOW-WELL SELF-PROPELLING BUCKET DREDGER

This vessel has an endless chain of buckets which can be lowered to the bottom of the river on an arm. For removing spoil, thus deepening the water. A hopper may or may not be incorporated in the hull. If not the spoil is shot into a separate hopper along-side.

DUMB BUCKET DREDGER

The working of this vessel is similar to that of the self-propelling types, but the hull is more box-shape, and she always shoots the spoil into a separate hopper. The dumb dredge must be towed to the site of her work— usually a dock or other enclosed water.

SIDE LADDER BUCKET DREDGER

Similar to other bucket dredgers, but has a ladder on each side. Chief advantage is her ability to dredge close to a dock wall or pier. On the other hand she is not so seaworthy and has more complicated mechanism. Very few of these have been built.

STERNWELL SELF-PROPELLING BUCKET DREDGER

This is another type of bucket dredger identical in working with the bow-well vessel, but the ladder is lowered between twin sterns. Having a normal bow shape she is probably the more seaworthy of the two. Like the bow-well vessel she may be either hopper or non-hopper.

DIPPER DREDGER

Movable arm, with large bucket at the end, is lowered to river bed. When raised, the whole crane-like structure may be swung round and the spoil deposited where required. Principle is similar to that of a 'Steam Navvy'. The dipper is most suitable for dredging in confined spaces.

GRAB DREDGER

Usually a small craft, particularly suitable for lifting spoil out of awkward corners. She may have any kind of hull: hopper, non-hopper, dumb or self-propelling, on which are mounted one or more deck cranes fitted with large grabs. The example is self-propelling and has four cranes.

PLACER DREDGER

Designed for recovering gold, platinum or tin from the beds of rivers or other water. A bucket ladder dredger with comparatively small buckets. The superstructure contains screening and other plant for the treatment of spoil. A large vessel may dredge to a depth of about 100 ft.

RECLAMATION DREDGER

Employed where land is being reclaimed.
Dredges up spoil and discharges it through
pipe line or conveyor. The discharge
mechanism is usually built into a lattice steel
arm which is swung out from the dredger,
allowing spoil to be deposited on the far side
of an embankment.

ROCK CUTTING DREDGER

Smashes rock for handling by ordinary
dredgers. Has a heavy ram with hard chisel
point. This is raised some distance off the
bottom and let fall in the manner of a pile
driver. The ram works either at one end of
the ship or through a well amidships.

SUCTION DREDGER

For working sand or soft mud, she has a
large pipe with a nozzle at the outer end,
which is lowered like the ladder of the bucket
dredger. In the hull are centrifugal pumps
which draw up the spoil. Some vessels have
revolving cutters on the nozzle for firm clay.

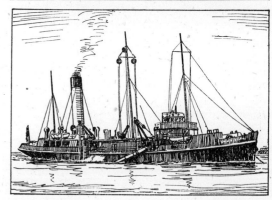

COAL ELEVATOR

This ugly but useful craft varies in design.
May be like illustration with self-propelling,
barge-shaped hull, or may be of pontoon type
more like the grain elevator. In the example
coal is sent from the hold up mechanical
conveyor, hence down a pivoted delivery
chute into the ship's bunkers.

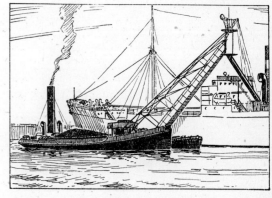

EXHIBITION SHIP

Vessel specially fitted out as a mobile exhibition of her owner's goods. Owing to the great expense incurred, few of these projects have been successful. The ship illustrated is an ex-passenger and cargo liner of 8,000 tons, whose purpose it was to visit foreign ports displaying British merchandise.

HARBOUR FIREFLOAT

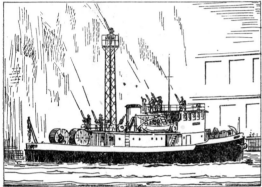

Most powerful of her type, this is a Diesel-electric vessel, 131 ft. × 32 ft., 9 ft. 3 in. draught. Propulsion controlled direct from pilot house. Four fire pumps are fitted, giving 20,000 gallons per minute. In communication with headquarters by wireless phone. Eight monitors are mounted, one on the lattice tower.

THAMES FIREFLOAT

Built for extinguishing fires in ships and riverside buildings. This vessel is a Diesel-engined, twin-screw boat with a speed of 12 knots. Fitted with a monitor and several hose connections served by powerful pumps. Her hull is designed to cause little wash. Dimensions: 78 ft. × 13 ft. 6 in. × 3 ft. 9 in. draught.

PONTOON CRANE

Used for lifting weights such as locomotives, lock gates, boilers, etc., in docks. Does not have to travel far so the hull is simply in the form of a flat box, although the example is self-propelled. Dimensions are: 201 ft. × 76 ft. × 8 ft. draught. She can lift about 150 tons.

SEA-GOING CRANE

The purpose of this vessel is identical with that of the pontoon crane, but she has a more ship-shape hull and is seaworthy enough to make coastal voyages from port to port under her own power. The illustration shows one of these ships on passage.

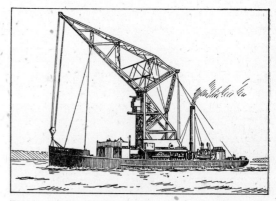

FLOATING DOCK

A hollow steel structure divided into water-tight compartments. These compartments are flooded until the dock is almost submerged. The ship is floated in, the compartments are pumped dry leaving ship and dock floor above water level. The floating dock may be towed from place to place. Used instead of drydock.

DANUBE FLOATING MILL

In out-of-the-way country districts of the River Danube, where there are many scattered farms, this unwieldy but useful craft travels from village to village turning the grain into flour. The vessel anchors in midstream where Danube's swift current turns water wheels on either side of the hull.

OCEAN FLYING-BOAT BASE

A modern ship type used as a refuelling and repairing depot on the German South Atlantic air route. She is fitted with catapulting apparatus for which the whole fore part is kept clear of obstruction. Also acts as a meteorological and radio station. Approximate dimensions : 245 ft. × 37 ft. 14 knots.

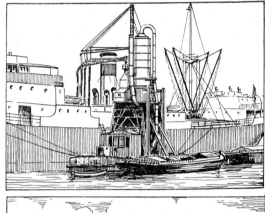

GRAIN ELEVATOR

An extraordinary-looking contraption used for discharging grain cargoes. The working part is mounted on a pontoon. It consists of an erection containing powerful air suction pumps and weighing machinery. Grain is sucked out of the ship on one side and discharged into barges on the other.

DUMB HOPPER

A steel vessel, the midship part of which is fitted with bottom doors. She is loaded with spoil from dredgers, towed to the dumping grounds, and when her doors are opened the spoil is released. The doors are operated by wires or chains taken over sheaves to winches on deck.

SELF-PROPELLING HOPPER

A sea-going vessel which carries spoil from dredger to dumping ground under her own power. Quite a few of these ships are over 200 ft. long, and have a spoil capacity of about 1,000 tons. They are fitted with bottom doors similar to those of the dumb hopper.

COALING HULK

In many cases all that remains of a once-famous sailing ship, the coal hulk is simply a grimy hull fitted with cranes. She is used as a depot in places where it is more convenient than shore equipment. An ignominious way for a proud ship to end her days.

I

POWDER HULK

One of those forlorn-looking craft to be seen moored in some desolate reach, miles from anywhere. The upper part of the hull and superstructure is painted bright red, and she flies a red flag. Hull usually all that remains of some obsolete vessel. Used for storage of explosives.

SHEER HULK

Before the introduction of floating cranes, ships were sometimes masted with the aid of a sheer hulk. This was a stout vessel with heavy mast amidships and sheer legs. The mast to be stepped was picked up by sheers and lowered into hole in the ship's deck alongside.

TRADING HULK

This type of depot ship, like the coal hulk, is usually a vessel which has come to the end of her seafaring career. Moored in some remote river, she acts as floating store and showroom for her company's goods. The example was, at one time, on the African West Coast.

ICE-BREAKER

A hefty ship designed and built to break channels through heavy ice for ordinary shipping. Hull of great strength with long, sloping forefoot to enable the ship to run up on the ice and crush it with her weight. Sometimes fitted with bow propeller. Average dimensions: 320 ft. × 70 ft.

KELEK

A strange craft from the River Tigris. Consists of a raft supported by inflated skins. Used for carrying cargo and passengers. For passengers a small hut is sometimes added. The vessel drifts with the current and is steered by long sweeps. Over 100 skins may be used to construct one Kelek.

LIGHTSHIP (Old Type)

Moored around the coasts, these craft act as floating lighthouses. In this type the mast passes through the lantern which may be lowered on deck for attention. May be distinguished one from another by various features such as cones, globes, etc., apart from name. Approximate dimensions : 100 ft. × 20 ft.

LIGHTSHIP (Modern Type)

In this type the lantern is mounted on a hollow steel tower. It can be attended to under cover and is in the form of a miniature lighthouse. Engines are fitted below, driving dynamo and foghorn. In addition many are fitted with wireless and submarine signalling apparatus.

LIVE BAIT CAGE

A contraption to store live fish used for bait. The example, from the Maldive Islands, is a basket 5 ft. × 3 ft. × 3 ft. 6 in. supported on either side by wooden floats. Moored in lagoon. A net is spread over to keep off sea birds. A similar cage is used in Japan.

MISSIONARY SHIP

According to date of building and particular station, individual ships differ a great deal. The vessel illustrated is a modern auxiliary schooner of 227 tons, working among the islands of the South Seas. Besides strictly mission work she carries stores, medical supplies, etc., and has room for some cargo.

NON-MAGNETIC SHIP

Built for study of magnetic and electrical phenomena which affect navigation, also of marine life. The hull is of teak on brass frames and a special Diesel engine of non-magnetic alloys is installed. Rigging, anchors, etc. are also of bronze or similar metal. Magnetic observatory and laboratory are fitted.

DISINFECTING PUNT

In natural public bathing lakes there is some danger of infection from the water. This craft is provided with cylinders of chemical gas which, combined with water, forms a powerful disinfectant. It is pumped out through pipes beside the keel. Motor boat, working at speed of about 3 knots.

SKELETON BOAT

Made like a crate of open slats so that the water can flow in and out. It is filled with young fish and towed from place to place during the re-stocking of rivers. A middle top section is removable for filling and emptying. Holds about 200 fish.

SLIPPER BOAT

Used as a floating home by the Tanka community of Canton. The interior is elaborately fitted out with every available comfort. These craft seldom have to be moved, and never for long distances, so one long oar, called a 'yuloh' is sufficient, worked over the stern. Dimensions about 25 ft. × 7 ft. 6 in.

OCEAN-GOING SAIL TRAINING SHIP

The majority of Naval Powers still train their officers in sailing or auxiliary vessels. The example, belonging to the Brazilian navy, has a displacement of 3,315 tons. Fitted with Diesel engines which give her 11 knots without sail. Very complete navigational equipment, small guns and other gear are installed.

TRAINING SHIP (Hulk)

An old vessel moored in a river or harbour for the training of naval or merchant service personnel. The example, of 4,725 tons displacement, is 214 ft. long. Good sleeping and school quarters. Electric lighting fitted. She has a number of boats used for rowing and sailing.

WEED CUTTER

Used on the Norfolk broads where weed becomes troublesome. Flat-bottomed, 20 ft. × 5 ft., driven by petrol engine working a stern wheel. The cutting blades are spring mounted so as to run over the river bottom without injury, and may be lowered to a depth of about 10 ft.

WRECK MARKING VESSEL

Employed by port authorities to mark position of craft sunk in or near the fairway. The drawing shows an ex-drifter owned by the Port of London. She is painted green and displays a large green flag to indicate to passing ships that she is standing by a wreck.

WRECK-RAISING VESSEL

Most ports possess wreck-raising craft. The best of these are handy little ships with a projection over the bows fitted with sheaves and lifting tackle. Extra large ballast tanks are provided to increase the lift. Powerful winches are fitted. Weight of craft lifted may exceed 100 tons.

OIL TANK BARGE

Employed in the transport of various kinds of oil and spirit, this craft is similar in appearance to the ordinary dumb barge or lighter, but the cargo space is divided into tanks with small, oil-tight hatches. Carries a square, red, metal flag to warn other vessels that she is carrying inflammable cargo.

FLOATING RESCUE STATION

Both British and Germans moored these craft at various points in the English Channel as refuges for airmen brought down in the sea. The British example has a metal hull, painted red and yellow. Provided with food, dry clothes, first-aid outfit, stove, etc. A wireless receiver, and signalling apparatus are included in the equipment.

GLOSSARY

ABAFT .... Behind or aft of.

AFT .... At or towards the stern.

AMIDSHIPS .... In the middle part of a ship, either longitudinally or trans-versely.

BALLAST .... Weight, in the form of water, iron, etc., put in the bottom of a ship to increase her stability.

BEAM .... The breadth of a vessel at her widest part.

BILGES .... The rounded off part of a ship's hull where the bottom meets the sides.

BILGE KEELS .... Keels fitted along bilges to reduce rolling or prevent damage when beaching.

BITTS .... Short posts, firmly secured to the deck, round which ropes are made fast.

BOOM .... A spar along the foot of a fore-and-aft sail.

BOW .... The forward end of a vessel.

BOWSPRIT .... Spar projecting from the bow to extend the headsails forward of the stem.

BRAILS .... Lines used for gathering a fore-and-aft sail in to the mast.

BULKHEAD .... A vertical partition between two compartments in a ship.

BULWARKS .... Solid, low walls around the sides of a ship above the deck.

BUMPKIN .... Stout spar projecting from a vessel's side or stern, such as a yawl uses for her mizen sheets.

CENTRE-PLATE .... A vertical plate, working in a slot through the bottom of a shallow-draught sailing vessel. Lowered as a temporary keel, reducing drift to leeward.

COAMINGS .... The built-up edges of hatches and other deck openings.

COUNTER .... The overhanging part of a vessel's stern.

CROW'S NEST.................. A fixed position built on a mast for the shelter of a lookout.

DAVITS .... Apparatus of various types for the swinging out and lowering of ship's lifeboats.

DERRICKS .... Wooden or tubular steel booms used for lifting cargo in and out of ship's holds.

DIESEL ENGINE .... A motor engine burning heavy oil in which the fuel mixture is exploded by pressure.

DISPLACEMENT .... The weight of water displaced by a ship, therefore the weight of the ship. Displacement tonnage is used for the measurement of war vessels.

DRAUGHT .... The depth of a vessel's keel below the surface of the water.

DUG-OUT .... Hollowed out of a single log.

FORECASTLE................... A compartment in the extreme bow, at one time invariably the crew's quarters.

GARBOARD STRAKE........ The line of planks or plating next to the keel.

GUNWALE...................... The upper edge of the sides of a boat.

HATCH .... An opening in the deck through which cargo is loaded into the hold of a ship.

HEADSAILS .... Fore-and-aft sails set between a vessel's foremost mast and the bowsprit or stem head.

LEEBOARDS .... Special pivoted boards fitted on either side of shallow-draught sailing craft to reduce drift to leeward.

LEEWARD .... The side or direction away from the wind.

LIST .... The tilting over of a ship to one side, such as may be caused by uneven distribution of weight.

LOOSE-FOOTED .... A sail, the foot of which is not laced to a boom.

LUGSAIL .... A fore-and-aft four-cornered sail on a yard, set in such a manner that about one-third of its length is before the mast.

MAST HOOPS .... Loose rings of wood round a mast to which the leading edge of a fore-and-aft sail is attached.

POOP .... The short raised deck at the stern of a ship.

QUARTER .... The part of a vessel's side near the stern.

RAKE .... The angle which masts, funnels, stem, etc., make with the perpendicular.

RECIPROCATING ENGINE — An engine which obtains its power by means of pistons working in cylinders.

RUBBING STRAKE .... Hard wooden band along a ship's sides to protect her from chafe against piers, etc.

SHEER .... The vertical curve in a vessel's deck line between bow and stern.

SHEER STRAKE .... The topmost continuous line of plating or planks along a ship's side.

SHEETS .... Lines by which a fore-and-aft sail is trimmed to take best advantage of the wind.

SHROUDS .... Ropes, usually wire, from the mast to the sides of a vessel, supporting the mast laterally.

SPOIL .... Mud, sand, etc., raised by dredgers.

SPRIT .... Heavy spar supporting a quadrilateral fore-and-aft sail without gaff or boom, as in the Thames Barge.

STAYS .... Standing rigging which supports the mast.

STEM .... A more or less vertical timber or casting forming the sharp edge of a vessel's bow.

STERN .... The after end of a vessel.

TABERNACLE .... A hinging arrangement at the foot of a mast allowing it to be lowered for negotiating bridges.

TACKING .... Steering a zig-zag course across the direction of the wind, heading the vessel as near as possible into the wind, thus making some headway against it on each tack.

THWARTS .... Seats fitted across a boat from side to side.

TILLER .... A steering bar attached to the rudder head.

TRANSOM STERN .... A flat, ' cut-off ' stern such as that of the 18th century ship's launch.

TUMBLE-HOME .... The part of a vessel's sides which slope inward from the waterline toward the deck.

TURBINE ENGINE .... An engine, the shaft of which is turned by steam passing through multi-bladed rotors.

WELL DECKS .... Short sections of the main deck which are open in some ships between the forecastle, bridge deck and poop. This is seen in the " Three Island " type of vessel.

YARDS .... Horizontal spars across a vessel's masts, on which square sails are set.

INDEX